Writers of Wales

EDITORS

MEIC STEPHENS   R. BRINLEY JONES

LEWIS JONES

1897–1939

David Smith

LEWIS

JONES

University of Wales Press
on behalf of the Welsh Arts Council

1982

I

At Christmas, 1929, Lewis Jones was thirty-one and about to enter a decade of unemployment. He scribbled on a blank, prefatory page of the diary he would keep for notes in 1930—*Minton, Chairman of Council offered Turkey. Refused it. Then offered fountain pen.* Lewis Jones would have found it hard to refuse any means of expression. Mere sustenance would be a secondary consideration for him. He was already a stormy figure in the virulent left-wing politics of his native Rhondda and, in the late 1920s, a convinced enemy of the 'social fascism' allegedly infecting the Labour party and his union, the South Wales Miners' Federation. He had been a member of the Communist Party since 1923. From 1925 to early 1930, he would act as a checkweighman at the Cambrian Colliery, Clydach Vale, on behalf of the miners who had elected him. By Christmas, 1938, he had led a number of hunger marches both out of and within South Wales; he had been elected as one of only two Communist County Councillors for Glamorgan in 1936. In a decade more renowned for its commentators on the working class than its working-class writers, this unemployed miner had become an acclaimed author of a lengthy novel, CWMARDY. He was now ardent in his support of unity, in a Popular Front, between Communists and Labour Party members, and tireless in his campaigning for aid for the beleaguered Spanish Republic. His second novel, WE LIVE, was almost completed. And then, in late January 1939, aged forty-one, he died, just before a decade he had lit up with his fervour expired in war.

His life had the taste of legend. There were grounds enough for it just in his youth allied to the intense nature of his abilities as an orator and writer. His secular funeral, winding its way through the packed streets of Tonypandy to Judge's Hall, seemed to symbolise the tragic hopes of 'red' Rhondda. His coffin had been draped in the scarlet banner stitched with gold leaf that women workers in Moscow had presented to A. J. Cook of the Rhondda in 1926 when he had gone, as General Secretary of the British Miners, to seek assistance from the Soviet Union during the agonising miners' lock-out of that year. Arthur Cook had, in turn, given it to the miners' lodge at Maerdy, Rhondda's 'Little Moscow', where Arthur Horner, Communist President of the South Wales Miners' Federation from 1936, was then checkweighman. A. J. Cook, himself only forty-seven, had died in 1931 as exhausted by political and industrial struggle as Lewis Jones would become. Now their mutual friend, Horner, flanked by leading figures in the public life of Rhondda, South Wales and Britain, declared: *We shall miss Lewis with his thought provoking ways, in the days that are to come.* The personal loss felt by those who had known an unusually warm, lively man was, perhaps, to be expected. His flame was kept

2

flickering by the posthumous publication of WE LIVE in 1939, followed by its re-print in 1941, but the years of silence, indeed ignorance, that surrounded his name were surely to follow naturally on the life of a man who never attained major public office, industrially or politically, and whose two novels could be quickly dismissed as honest, but clumsy, examples of the 1930s working-class epic.

Nonetheless, when the social and political history of the coalfield began, in the 1960s, to receive serious attention from historians Lewis Jones's importance was quickly made apparent. Appeals for the re-printing of his novels were made from the early 1970s. What was, initially, surprising is that Lewis Jones now took on another resonance, contemporary again for those who 'discovered' him, that, in some ways, outstrips his fame of the late 1930s. He even takes on a fictional form as the sexually dynamic (somewhat unscrupulous) Pen Lewis, Communist militant and opponent of idealistic nationalism, in Emyr Humphreys' 1978 novel, THE BEST OF FRIENDS. Undoubtedly, Lewis Jones, the man and orator, had an emblematic function in late twentieth-century Welsh life.

The occasional literary attention that he had attracted before this accorded only a certain rooted authenticity to his fiction but now he was to be interpreted more generously outside the canon of mainstream literature. More than this, his attempt to write narrative prose about a collective working-class experience was seen by some as a central, neglected endeavour, for all its stumbling failures, and by others as a major

3

conceptual breakthrough in the twentieth-century novel. Clearly Lewis Jones's two novels presented a different working-class world than either Jack Jones or Richard Llewellyn did in the 1930s—Raymond Williams considered that Lewis Jones moved the focus of a traditional novel form out of the family and towards 'a cause and . . . a party' (THE WELSH INDUSTRIAL NOVEL, Cardiff 1978) whilst Carole Snee believed that, after the traditionalism of CWMARDY, Lewis Jones . . . *in his treatment of women, of the working class, and of personal relationships . . . breaks with the liberal ideology which has for so long surrounded and helped define the realist novel form, and in* WE LIVE *in particular he begins to explore ways of opening up the form to allow the introduction of a proletarian consciousness* (CULTURE AND CRISIS IN BRITAIN IN THE THIRTIES, 1979). Lewis Jones, therefore, was to be placed firmly within a European context of writing and criticism (specifically a Marxist perspective, generally an innovative or struggling one) in which his 'faults' of construction and presentation could be seen as the product of genuine intellectual and aesthetic difficulty as much as deriving from his own apprentice stage. To European scholars of the 'proletarian novel', especially those in Germany, Denmark and Spain, Lewis Jones's neglect in Wales was surprising. The re-printing of his novels in soft-cover form in 1978 won him an extremely wide, appreciative audience; critics began to offer more straight-forward affirmations of his intrinsic literary skills. At the very least it was established that there was room for critical disagreement over the precise nature of his achievement. For David Smith (in SOCIALIST PROPAGANDA IN THE 20TH CENTURY BRITISH NOVEL (1978)) Lewis Jones had *few, if any, of the novelist's gifts* whereas John Pikoulis (in an essay of 1981) claimed him *as one of the finest of modern British novelists [and] one of the most neglected.*

At first sight his career as a political agitator is less contentious. After all there was no compromise of the middle-aged or disillusioned in *his* public life. He had suffered a heart attack after spending all day addressing scores of street corner meetings in the cause of the Spanish Republic. This final sacrifice was all of a piece with the earlier determination that had led to his imprisonment for 'sedition' in 1926 and to a number of court appearances for 'inciting disorder' in the 1930s. In the winter of 1978–9 at the special Day School, and subsequent series of meetings, under the title 'The Lewis Jones Lectures' (organised by *Llafur:* The Society for the Study of Welsh Labour History), the memory which old friends and political comrades invoked was one of ceaseless dedication allied to very special gifts of communication. About the latter there could be no doubt. They added to his romantic carelessness for self, the lustre of compassion and the fire of rhetorical anger. His voice, an essential tool of the orator's trade in pre-microphone days, was light but well-modulated, able to play on a range of emotions: it had a slight break, a catch, in it. During the 1926 lock-out he gave a number of talks (lectures would be too formal a word) on any number of subjects to enthusiastic audiences. They lasted anything up to two and a half hours at a time. On the other hand, his close involvement with his particular community allowed him, in the middle of perorations against the iniquity of the Unemployment Regulations in the mid-1930s, to interrupt himself to ask named individuals whether or not he was telling a general truth as it affected them in their daily lives. Wit, and a constant, railing mockery of the attendant police who dogged his footsteps and mangled his words, was added like a spice to speeches that never patronised, yet never soared above, an audience so severely afflicted by social deprivations that he would start gently before easing his and their way to an analysis of the working-class plight he was resolved to expose. This short, slight, fair-haired man, with an almost cherubic pudginess, took no account of the routine of mealtimes, normal patterns of life (despite an early marriage) or social conventions. Confronted by personal cases of hardship, whether on the street or behind closed doors, he would not suppress his emotions but, sometimes embarassingly, break down in tears of rage or frustration and pity. Allied to this ability to identify with the most miserable parts of his community, the long-term unemployed, was the resolution, and organisational drive, that saw him lead Hunger Marches to London in 1932, 1934 and 1936. No wonder, then, that this doomed, charismatic figure who, in the words of an old friend who became a novelist (Gwyn Thomas), *shunned the velvet summits,* should attract a direct response from different generations in a way that a figure blunted by trade union bureaucracy or whittled away by political shuffling could not hope to do.

Even so, this justifiable celebration of the man masks a more fascinating ambiguity which, (as with his novels, rough *and* delicate at the same time), is the source of his magnetism. There was about Lewis Jones, Gwyn Thomas remembered privately, *a sort of bright slyness* that was in marked contrast to the *unrelenting, dour Cromwellianism* of other leading Communists in South Wales. There were seven Communist councillors, local and county, from the Rhondda in 1936. They were duly memorialised, as a sizeable minority, in a group photograph. Lewis Jones stood slightly apart, to the left of the group, quizzical and quite distinct. He wears, unlike the others, neither waistcoat nor tie nor watch fob nor smile. His shirt has its soft collar typically open and from the top pocket of a shiny double-breasted suit a rather cavalier handkerchief flaunts itself. He adopted penury as a style, almost projecting himself boldly as a physical emblem of widespread poverty that might otherwise stay sullen and hidden. It was, at times, a bravura personal performance that gave others hope. He was aware of the transitoriness of sheer pleasure in the lives around him and, by openly snatching at it himself, avoided the sanctimoniousness of 'holier' lives. His *thought provoking ways* often provoked, during his lifetime, those whose public and private conduct was more adamantine, more in keeping with the exemplary role required of leaders of *the coming revolutionary struggle*. In the summer of 1930 he wrote in his diary—*Jack called up re: my apathy* (a reference to his close friend, Jack Jones, who would fight in Spain as an International Brigader) and, two weeks later, *Sign* (for unemployment benefit) *2.15. Went on Randy.* It was a tendency to avoid the disciplining agencies of domesticity, teetotalism and regularity, in food and dress, that made political associates smile ruefully or shake their heads in disapproval. At his funeral, Harry Pollitt, General Secretary of the Communist Party of Great Britain, observed that this advocate of *the common people* had not been *one of nature's gentlemen*. Nor did Lewis Jones restrain his disruptive conduct within personal bounds. At several points he clashed with authority inside the Communist Party which responded to his erratic, unreliable behaviour by suspending him or removing him from key positions. Perhaps the most stunning episode in his maverick political life came when he attended, as a British delegate, the Seventh World Congress of the Communist International in the Soviet Union in 1935. A fellow delegate is sure that Lewis Jones's gesture was no personal aberration and that it went beyond his dislike of the Congress, his distaste for the round of speeches and the obvious way in which, like a rebellious schoolboy, he took refuge in beneath-the-desk literature whilst platform speakers rattled on. Indeed, his closest confidante of those years, the woman who part-wrote and saw the final chapters of WE LIVE through the press, Mavis Llewellyn, recalled that he wrote from Moscow declaring his deep feelings of unease before the cult of leadership then being propagated. She affirmed that his refusal to stand or clap for the person or name of Joseph Stalin was neither unexpected nor inconsistent.

It never seems to have occurred to Lewis Jones that his conduct might just not be politic. It was unthinkable not to be political and he never wavered from his commitment to the Communist Party as the most advanced section of the working class; though, like Arthur Horner, his insistence on also adding his own views to the current party line did not always endear him to those who were, first and foremost, party organisers. So the legend and the man are better melted back the one into the other so that this extraordinary life can be seen as revelatory of an active, rounded response to the packed history of the South Wales coalfield. A great deal of the evidence for that life is either secondary and tangential (newspaper reports, brief articles, letters to newspapers, two attenuated diaries of brief notes and memoranda) or a rich, conflicting mixture of reminiscence and tribute (interviews, broadcasts, lectures) that separate their subject out by highlighting. He presents the unusual case, therefore, of a writer who has left very little direct account of himself or his intentions and of a politician whose control was not over committees or agenda but over crowds and the philosophy of crowds. He was, thought Gwyn Thomas, *like explosive in the mind . . . a high priest of self-expression . . . who was constantly hinting at our need to deepen our wisdom, our sophistication . . . that we must cease to be simple.* And in this he is markedly akin to another South Walian, also born in 1897, who used his people's *cult of the word* as a weapon: for Aneurin Bevan's power to shape a sense of reality also resided in his willingness to catch fire from his community, to risk the moment on a turn of phrase or instinctive gesture. This made, in both of them, for structural flaws as well as fleeting triumphs; the meaning of both men can only be grasped within the context of that coalfield culture and community which mostly made them. It was a reciprocal process that

Lewis Jones attempted to show in his novels. For all their fictional attributes, they may come to be seen as a valiant imaginative exploration of the social reality which underpinned his own spinning life.

II

Lewis Jones was born on 28 December 1897 in the mid-Rhondda. His mother Jane, who survived him, was a domestic servant. He was illegitimate and, in an almost literal sense, a child of the coalfield itself. He was brought up, largely by his grandmother, in Blaenclydach at the top end of the steep cwm that rises up from Tonypandy Square. He lived all his life in Clydach Vale which is, for the most part, the setting of his novels. Attendance at elementary school was punctuated by frequent absences in which he lived a street life in an attempt to add to the household income. Formal schooling was ended by work in the pit when he was twelve. There was nothing unusual in this pattern nor in his early marriage in 1917. However, there was no better vantage point than mid-Rhondda from which to view and assess the explosive pattern of South Welsh life. He went to work in the Cambrian Colliery which was a cornerstone of the group of pits known as the Cambrian Combine. They had been brought together in an act of advanced capitalist rationalisation by D. A. Thomas, Liberal MP for Merthyr and, from 1909, for Cardiff, himself the clearest thinker amongst an antediluvian bunch of coalowners. D. A. Thomas, as recalled by the Clydach Vale born (1903) novelist Rhys Davies, would ride through the village to the pit like some haughty conquistador. When he died in 1918 he had taken the generic

11

name, Lord Rhondda. Lewis Jones would sketch him as Lord Cwmardy.

Within a year of his starting work the Cambrian Combine strike embroiled all of the mid-Rhondda pits in a year long dispute that ended in defeat for the men. They caught international attention early on, in November 1910, when the strike led to the riots at Tonypandy and the dispatch of troops. The thirteen year old collier boy would have seen all this; the novelist would alter events for his purpose. That purpose, or insight, was formed not only by the rush of spectacular events but also by the informed judgements that he was able to absorb from older men. Mid-Rhondda was a centre for the 'advanced men' of the coalfield. They were sometimes identified as 'syndicalists', sometimes as 'industrial unionists', always as 'socialists'. They shared in common ideas about the direct power that could be exerted by an organised working class (perhaps via a general strike, maybe through the ballot box) in order to win workers' control of their industry (for some without the state, for others through nationalisation), and hence gain control of the state itself. There was a Marxian club in Clydach Vale, associated with the Social Democratic Federation, and leading members of the Cambrian Lodge had attended, on miners' supported scholarships, the adult education college, Ruskin College at Oxford. Then, from 1909, they supported the students' strike that eventually led to the setting up, with SWMF backing, of the specifically Marxist-orientated Central Labour College. Noah Rees, check-weigher and lodge secretary at the Cambrian

Colliery, a major influence in the 1910–11 strike, was such a man—resolute, principled and ultimately a convinced pragmatist. Many of his traits would be incorporated into the character of Ezra in the novels. The root and branch activities of the Central Labour College were carried out through the Plebs League which had as a local representative another Cambrian Lodge activist, the future Rhondda MP, W. H. Mainwaring, an earnest intellectual pedagogue who would become a lecturer at the Central Labour College in London from 1919 to 1924 (during Lewis Jones's time there). These two spearheaded the local thrust of the Unofficial Reform Committee, established to agitate for rank and file control of the SWMF, and were prominent amongst the authors of the 'collective' pamphlet THE MINERS' NEXT STEP. This document, published in Tonypandy in 1912, was quickly circulating throughout the British coalfields where, in that year, a national strike won a minimum wage for coalminers. The educational classes organised by these men, and by their ally, the Maerdy checkweighman, Noah Ablett, were attended by the youthful Lewis Jones who, during the war, would see a government brought to bay through the unofficial strike action of over 200,000 South Welsh miners. His own studies to be a mining engineer dwindled in the face of his developing interest in political philosophy. His appetite was supplied by the well stocked library in the Workmen's Institute and a blossoming vocabulary was tried out within the mass meetings of the Lodge. Before the War had ended he was the youngest Chairman that the Cambrian Lodge had ever elected.

The optimistic militancy fuelled by the ever-rising demand for coal in the war now foundered on post war economic recession. There were bitter disputes and strikes, nationally and locally, from 1919 to 1924. Mass unemployment began to settle in. In 1923 Lewis Jones went, on a scholarship established by his fellow workmen, to the Labour College. Here he seems to have widened his reading, especially of literature, but to have been less interested in the formal study of Marxist economics and philosophy. Aneurin Bevan who had preceded Lewis Jones at the College (1919–21) enjoyed the same reputation for late night disputes, late rising, absenteeism and a preference for speechifying around London. Lewis Jones's stay overlapped with that of his friend Jack Jones, on whom his main fictional character Len Roberts is partly based, and it coincided with that of Idris Cox, from the Llynfi Valley, who would, from 1927, be Communist Party organiser in South Wales. Lewis Jones joined the CP during his stay in London which was cut short, by a few months, in 1925 when he returned to the Rhondda. The premature move was impelled in part by family financial considerations. He had also been involved in a fractious dispute at the Cambrian Colliery, in late 1923 and early 1924, as management attempted to remove customary rights, alter working methods and 'choose' their employees. It was at this point that Noah Rees, advocating caution and compromise, was denounced by more militant leaders in terms that marked a final political breach. On his return Lewis Jones was elected a checkweighman at the Cambrian Colliery by the men. Noah Rees, who had been made a JP in 1919, died aged sixty-four in 1934.

His protégé's political activity accelerated as the industrial crisis between owners, men and government headed for the General Strike of 1926. Lewis Jones, along with others, was instructed by the Communist Party to go to Nottinghamshire where the unity of the strike was threatened by a break-away non-political association headed by the right-wing coalminers' MP for the area, George Spencer. From late 1926 the Spencer Union, commonly known in South Wales as a 'company' or 'scab' union of the 'non-pols', had a South Wales twin in the South Wales Miners' Industrial Union. This was finally driven out of the coalfield in 1938, but only after the dramatic device of 'stay-down' strikes, in which SWMF men occupied the pits, had been devised to counter the 'blackleg' problem. This was a crucial episode in the re-building of the SWMF after the destruction, to both membership and morale, wrought by the defeat of 1926. Lewis Jones would give it due prominence in WE LIVE.

His own life seemed, for a time, to be intertwined with these struggles of the unemployed. His dramatic rallying speeches in Nottinghamshire led to allegations of sedition which pursued him back home. He continued to offend against the Emergency regulations by urging 'disaffection' and was duly sentenced to three months hard labour in Swansea jail. The life of a known Communist militant was not an easy one in the atmosphere of malice and victimisation that now hung over the coalfield. From 1928 there were deep divisions within the SWMF itself as the old alliance of progressives in the Unofficial Reform Movement separated further into mutually hostile groups based around the 'evolutionary' Labour Party and the 'revolutionary' Communist Party (founded in 1920). Recriminations were fierce. The CP in particular now argued that only the destruction of the official Labour Party could allow the revolutionary potential of the workers to be released. Those Communists who expressed doubts about the wisdom, leave alone practicality, of this schematic policy were, in turn, pilloried. Between 1930 and 1932 Arthur Horner, South Wales' outstanding Communist, on whom Lewis Jones draws for the character of Harry Morgan, was accused of internal opposition. Lewis Jones, in common with other Communists still connected to the SWMF (itself now denounced as a hopelessly reactionary organisation), expressed their grave doubts. His own lodge underwent, in the words of his diary for January 1930, a 'clean sweep' on the committee by 'right-wingers'. This brought to a head his earlier refusal to weigh coal cut by men he considered 'blacklegs' because of their action in the post-1926 period, and caused his removal, in a depleted, demoralised colliery, as checkweighman. These were, compared to the hopeful days before 1926 and the re-emergent activism after 1934, grim, uncertain years in which he seems, for a time, to have lessened his involvement. The forceful coalfield community which had, through men and women like himself, begun to look for control of its future had, by the late 1920s, smashed on the rocks of economic misery. Social despair and loss of political direction threatened South Wales.

.

16

None were more threatened than the unemployed. The short-time, temporary unemployment of trade recessions, or the sort that had come in the aftermath of disputes, now gave way to a cancerous invasion of the whole society. There were many black spots in an area where no valley or town was free of blight. In the Rhondda the percentage unemployed in the insured workforce rose from 2% in 1923 to 20% in 1929 to over 40% by 1937. At that date 63% of those unemployed had been out of work for an average period of five years. Lewis Jones, moving through the rounds of rallies, back room meetings and lectures, found his cause in the appalling circumstances of an unemployed society. The threat was not only psychological, or even physical, for the vast army of workless, if left alone, abandoned by their wider community, might swing haphazardly as a political force. Early in the 1920s the National Unemployed Workers' Movement, spurred on by the Communist Party, had begun to organise activities to counter voluntarist, or philanthropic, movements in the depressed areas. Lewis Jones asked himself at the end of his diary in 1930 under the title 'Notes for 1931'—*Is Communist policy beneficial to the Working Class?* His answer must have been affirmative for he acted as election agent that year for the Communist candidate in Rhondda West and he became the principal NUWM organiser in South Wales.

His fame as a speaker of startling, unorthodox powers spread beyond the Rhondda to neighbouring valleys where he would go on speaking tours, in halls and outside labour exchanges, for days at a time. The intention in the early 1930s was to exert pressure upon the Labour-dominated urban and county councils, by marching to the authorities in charge of dispensing relief, and to force the government (a National one, dominated by the Tories after the 1931 election) to take notice of the protests of the unemployed. The marches were disciplined occasions, with poor equipment but dedicated participants. The small scale affairs of 1930 and 1931 progressed, via several inter-coalfield demonstrations in 1932, to a march in 1933, from upper Monmouthshire to Newport, which won the adherence of 500 marchers and, in a county with 40,000 unemployed, brought crowds ranging from 20,000 to 50,000 onto the streets. Lewis Jones was the principal organiser of these pleas for better treatment from the Public Assistance Committees of the elected authorities.

The government in 1934 decided to tidy up anomalies in the system of unemployment relief by removing such dispensation from elected officials. Unemployment Assistance Boards, with new, regularised rates of relief, operating a stricter Means Test, were to be set up. That year the NUWM marchers' council organised its biggest march from South Wales to London and as the 'unemployed question' finally registered itself as 'a working-class question' the years of agitation paid off in an increased revulsion against the policy. From early 1935 the major political, industrial and social organisations in the coalfield began to work together, as their rank and file members had already been doing, on common platforms. The result was huge, community demonstrations, running into hundreds of thou-

18

sands of people, which actually made the government retract. These mass demonstrations were quite orderly. However, there had been fierce clashes with the police at a number of spots in 1934, whilst in February 1935 the UAB office at Merthyr was invaded by 3,000 people, led by the NUWM, who destroyed the assembled files. This episode, and his experiences in general, are weaved into the defiant pages of WE LIVE.

When the government's amended, and considerably improved regulations, were being prepared for introduction in 1936 Lewis Jones was again one of the leaders of a march to London which united all sections of his battered society. By this time he was an old local council campaigner, too. He narrowly missed election on a number of occasions to the Rhondda UDC but won a seat on the Glamorgan County Council in Spring 1936. The Communist Party was well rooted once more within the SWMF and fully set on its Popular Front policy, calling for united action by all socialists and democrats against the threat of fascism. It was the kind of atmosphere, hopeful and heroic, charged with the possibilities of open, mass action, that Lewis Jones had experienced before 1926, and to which he now gave his apparently inexhaustible energies. Nothing deterred him, not even being bound over for 12 months (and breaking sureties for an earlier offence) in 1937 when he was alleged to have warned unemployment officers that he would bring a demonstration to their doors if they did not heed the complaints of the unemployed.

The 1936 March to London was greeted by a

number of Labour MPs, including Aneurin Bevan who had had close links with Communists like Arthur Horner and Lewis Jones throughout the 1930s. Bevan would soon be temporarily expelled from his party for his advocacy of closer links within a Popular Front movement. Lewis Jones, for all his popularity, had already fallen out of step with the CP in 1935. His waywardness, with matters of policy and of organisation, continued to dog his steps in the late 1930s though without dissipating the euphoria in which he worked at a feverish pace. The only dents in his armour were the searing anger and the uncontrollable pity he experienced as European conflict sucked the world, and his friends, into war. At the rally of 60,000 people in Tonypandy which sent the 1936 contingent of Rhondda hunger marchers on their way he had drawn attention to the revolt of the generals which had occurred ten days before in Spain. Lewis Jones would himself volunteer to serve in the International Brigades in Spain. He would be rejected by the CP, mostly for his propagandist value at home, partly for reasons of health and partly because he was not thought fitted for the hard-line work of a political commisar that another Rhondda unemployed leader, Will Paynter, undertook. In the meantime he saw younger comrades from his village and his pit go to Spain to be imprisoned, to die, maybe to survive. He collapsed in January 1939 (in the week Barcelona, the last real Republican hope, fell to Franco) thinking that Jack Jones, who had been imprisoned, would never return. He had already planned a third book, maybe a novel or perhaps a play, in which the triumphant return of the International Brigaders from Spain would mark the resurrection of a popular, revolutionary impulse at home. Mavis Llewellyn, a schoolteacher in the Ogmore valley, with whom he had discussed the projected ending of WE LIVE, was left to complete the last one and a half chapters.

Her advice had been sought earlier to smooth his form and style because the books Lewis Jones managed to write had, as he explained in the Preface to CWMARDY, been *written during odd moments stolen from mass meetings, committees, demonstrations, marches and other activities*. The impulse to write the first novel had, according to the author, been sparked off by *my friend and comrade Mr. Arthur Horner . . . [who] . . . suggested that the full meaning of life in the Welsh mining areas could be expressed for the general reader more truthfully and vividly if treated imaginatively, than by any amount of statistical and historical research.* (Preface CWMARDY). The interesting phrases are 'the full meaning of life' and 'treated imaginatively' because they imply that neither the flood of government reports commissioned on the coalfield down to 1936, as well as the massive SECOND INDUSTRIAL SURVEY in three volumes that was to come in 1937, nor the works of documentary reportage with quasi-sociological leanings had conveyed the tenor of life in a region which, in common with other sites of industrial dereliction, was fascinating outside observers by the mid-1930s. That decade had, of course, produced 'working-class' novels already. In Wales, Jack Jones's 1934 book, RHONDDA ROUNDABOUT, a panorama of vignettes that amounted to 'faction', had been greeted eagerly and even performed on the West End stage; Gwyn Jones's youthful novel

TIMES LIKE THESE, essentially an account of the General Strike period, would appear in 1936. Rhys Davies, who lived in the Rhondda until the 1920s, though far more impressionistic in his treatment of South Walian life, was another writer of whom Lewis Jones would have been aware. And from Communist newspapers and reviews he would know of attempts to encourage schools of 'worker novelists' in Europe and the USA. Despite this flurry of interest there were no ready models to which a tyro novelist could turn for depictions of collective, communal life from which the individual did not recoil or escape but in which individual life had to be rooted. This was Lewis Jones's political and social creed based, as he thought, on the reality of his observation. This was for him the meaning of a 'phase of working class history' that he set out 'to "novelise" '.

Serious work on CWMARDY may have begun in late 1935 in periods of the enforced lull after his suspension by the Communist Party in South Wales. Certainly it was well under way through 1936 because the second note-diary that survives records a swift progress through 1937. The early days of January are punctuated by the instructions 'Sign 9.15' (for the dole) or 'Cases 10–12' (advising others) but marked consistently by the words 'Book', 'Book', 'Book', until these extracted entries which in their brevity, energy and circum-scribed drama seem to encapsulate his life. On other days, scattered amongst them, are continual references to street meetings, relief committee cases, lectures and public demonstrations:

January 13	*Finished Book.*
January 14	M.T. (Means Test) *man called.* *Sent final manuscript away.*
January 20	*Sign 9.15. Trial at Pontypridd. Bound for two years. £2.10s. (fine).*
January 21	*Typing all day. Prep. draft ground work new book.*
January 22	*Film. Sign 9.15.*
January 29	*Sign 9.15. Start on book.*
February 9	*On book all night.*
March 1	*Polling Day* C.C. (County Council). *630 maj.*
March 5	*Means test men called. Summons Bridgend.*
March 12	*Bridgend police court.*
March 26	*Proofs done.*
April 5	*Book* (started again).
April 8	*Spain meeting. Book.*
April 15	*Fined in Bridgend court.*
June 17	*Received first copy of Book.*
June 21	*Book published.*
June 23	*Measured for suit.*

The last entries for December read 'Book', 'Book', 'Put in coal.'

Being a collier was what made Lewis Jones a writer. It was writing, or, at first, articulation of experiences through public speech, that allowed Lewis Jones the means of making sense both of his, and his community's, being. There were ready made clichés to hand. Some of these were political, others merely rhetorical. It was no easy task to tread a path through these snares. In his public career Lewis Jones had found the courage to be mistaken in the eyes of the already convinced. In his speeches he obviously found the

23

means of avoiding the ready expectation, the smug sense of completion. An enduring strength of his novels is their willingness to spread their nets wide despite the specific intention in his use of the novel form i.e. that it should act as a more effective explanation of the necessary politicisation of the coalfield.

To this end his very early writing is earnestly didactic. The short stories he contributed to the DAILY WORKER in 1932 are revolutionary homilies of the type much in evidence during the Communist Party's 'third Period' of 'class against class'. The force of material reality will convince the workers of their exploitation. The scales of illusion will fall from their eyes; illumination follows; the trumpet-note of revolution must sound. The two stories ('Young Dai' and 'Power of the Pit') waste little time in building to their point. The narrator's voice is one-toned. The message of the story we hear about Dai is that the war between nations which crippled him is giving way, in his nephew's day, to the war between classes that, alone, can end war. It is Dai's own experience that teaches a new generation. The story ends with the slogans this knowledge has produced ('*Down with the warmongers, the mutilators of our class*') but it is the specific detail which holds our attention.

We didn't see him after till about 1917 when we met him as we were going home from work one day. The street was all beflagged to welcome him, and the night before he went back we had a fine smoking concert and booze up in his honour.

It was a long time after the war when we came across him

24

again. He had been to hospital. Something the matter with his legs.

He started back in the pit in 1921. Didn't work long though. Trouble with his legs.

They took him to hospital. Doctors were interested in his case. They couldn't make out what was wrong with his legs.

Took both of them off after nine operations to see what was wrong . . . .

We lost him then until the latter end of 1927, when we saw him sliding up the street on a flat board, with a piece of stick in each hand to drag himself along. His two legs were off at his hips.

He told us the military doctors had at last agreed. He was not entitled to pension because 'his legs were predisposed to gangrene'.

We clubbed up in the pit and brought him a little carriage; artificial legs were no use because he had been amputated too high up.

On the other hand 'Power of the Pit' discards both compassion for individual tragedy and irony in its telling. It is a 'mass' story Lewis Jones wishes to express about the power of the pit. He resorts to repetitive rhetoric, in the time-honoured style of the platform orator (*Red was the colour of the blood they lost. Red is the colour of the revolution they will make*), and to a metaphor whereby the pit becomes 'the monster' which 'screamed and shouted . . . for its human meal'. The lesson here is that the pit, in its days of demise, can be turned into the salavation of unemployed workers provided we 'take it for ourselves'. Both these sketches, published at a time when the Communist Party as well as militant rank and file miners were actually in considerable disarray in the coalfield, end with an optimistic certainty that victory, based on the sacrifice and enlightenment of the past, will soon come.

As unemployment continued to rise and as neither the official trade union movement nor its left-wing critics proved able to halt the decline in wage rates and the rise in non-unionism, so it became clearer that past understanding had to be directly related to the crisis of the present if it were to inform future direction. Within South Wales Arthur Horner, so recently vilified by the CP for his supposed lack of faith in the revolutionary readiness of the people, took up a leading role, along with Idris Cox, in establishing the Communist rank and file fortnightly newspaper THE SOUTH WALES MINER in June 1933. This urged miners to re-join and re-build the South Wales Miners Federation. By the end of the year Horner, who had been virtually excluded from union activity since 1930 and who had been in jail from August to December 1932, now symbolised the resurrection of a more traditional, more circumspect policy by being elected as a miners' agent in West Wales. This progress was more cautious than it was heroic but it owed its success to a resolution and realism that would not be easily dismissed.

Lewis Jones's two DAILY WORKER stories of 1933 begin to reflect this new mood and, at the same time, extend his technical range. In particular, the characters he depicts respond to their respective fates in more complex fashion. Courage and comradeship remain his human staples without becoming the automatic agents of political and social betterment. Clearly, his writing did not alter totally nor simply shift in accord with the switch in tactics and strategy (neither completed by mid-1933 anyway). Nevertheless, the greater subtlety apparent in his prose is connected to a willingness to present the political enemy as more insidiously powerful and those who require leadership as caught in the trap of their own horrors. The would-be political leader, then, needs the true heroism of patience. His story, ' "Boots, Shiny, Big and Heavy" ' attempts to show exactly this by depicting a Communist militant, isolated and not a little afraid, awaiting trial. The contrast between the injustice meted out to him and the overheard newsvendor's cries about the torture and lack of a public trial suffered by an Englishman in Moscow is, again, rather forced as a device. What is quite compelling, though, is the prisoner's hypnotic obsession with the boots of the police—*Better than batons when a man was down*—and the account of the social composition of the magistrates' Bench. Between this brute force and this social vice he must be crushed. His spirit is, for all that, not cowed by a jail sentence for he is aware, by their singing outside, that *his comrades were near and that he was not alone despite his cage with its bodyguard of blue.*

Two months later, in June 1933, he published 'The Pit Cage'. It is a startlingly graphic vignette about a pit cage ('the last bond') crashing two thousand feet to pit bottom. Once more he moves inside emotions to probe imaginatively rather than simply vent his savage indignation. And, as will happen in his novels, the terrible force of a particular event in his fiction will show its bruise directly:

They did not see the smashed and shattered sides, the matchsticks made in an instant from the six-inch oak planks that used to cover the pit bottom, the tangle of steel threads that was once a two-inch wire rope, the little bits of iron that had been 30 feet girders. They saw none of these things. Someone lived. Someone was calling for help.

'Oh, mam.'

Carefully, patiently they tugged and pulled and probed and carried . . . They knew each one by his clothes. Fingers slipped in blood, flesh clung in lumps to tender hands.

'Careful, boys, careful.' One by one. Side by side. Fractured limbs, smashed heads, shattered bodies . . . Fourteen of them.

Everyone twenty seconds before had been a man, had seen the daylight snatched from him as if by a gigantic hand. Only twenty seconds. And now four were left breathing. The others had legs driven up through their bodies by the impact, backbones smashed till they seeped through ghastly holes like jelly squeezed through a sieve . . . 'Steady, boys.'

His own public role as tribune for the unemployed went hand in hand with his personal identification with all the evils suffered by the people he tried to represent in his politics and in his writing. Just as he could publish (in the LEFT REVIEW in 1937) an excerpt from CWMARDY under the title 'Tonypandy' so, in his journalism and pamphlets, he would try to demonstrate the interaction of the individual and the social, the public and the private, of 'fact' and 'fiction'. Writing in two modes allowed him to experiment with a mix of close-ups and panoramic long-shots that he would eventually fuse into a style equipped to handle the formidable problems he would set himself in the conception and execution of the novels. Meanwhile, in 1934 and in

1935, the quasi-fiction of 1932 and 1933 was replaced by the dramatic, interventionist pamphlets inspired by the facts and actions of his contemporary South Wales. A short piece, entitled 'The Rhondda in 1934', sustains a teasing juxtaposition of daily suffering at the hands of the courts, the police, the coalowners and the Council itself with the fact that 'Labour has ruled for ten years'. Earlier, intemperate accusations of 'social fascism' have given way to contemptuous dismissal of Labour's administration. His journalism at this time, brief and vigorous, is mostly concerned to nurture the power it senses stirring once more in the people in *a working class that has proved its fighting courage in dozens of actions, and which is straining at the Labour leash holding it in temporary check.*

Political energies were now focussed on mobilising mass protests against the suffocating immobility of bureaucracies. The attack proceeds, in this logic, against the National Government's regulations, and against Labour authorities who fail to reject them, at the epicentre of their effect—the local level. Lewis Jones's writing bristles with confident energy in the two extended pamphlets and in a SOUTH WALES SLAVE ACT SPECIAL (an eight page paper) which he wrote, in the gaps he found between intense political activism, from 1933 to 1935.

The first pamphlet concerns the march organised by the NUWM within Monmouthshire in August 1933 and, ostensibly, was 'written and compiled' by members of the Monmouthshire Marchers Council with only a foreword by Lewis Jones. Nonetheless, the dramatic vivacity of the prose

which breaks up a statistical marshalling of the
care for the unemployed by means of a lively
blow-by-blow account of the march, indicates
the hand of the future novelist. The historic
present tense has, perhaps, an over-insistent
cinematic quality but it builds effectively to the
required confrontation of marchers and councillors. The political point is that only 'mass
action' can win just demands, for the elected
Labour leaders will, it is alleged, inevitably
succumb to 'anti-working class influences'. At its
conclusion Lewis Jones effectively hammers home
the issue in a run of ringing contrasts:

*The demands of the Marchers are the programme around
which all decent elements are mobilising. Only the ignorant,
the depraved, the cynical, the rich and the Labour leaders are
against the demands. We are many; they are few. A mad
world, mass expenditure on armaments as preparation for mass
world slaughter. Decrease of births. Granaries full of grain:
storehouses full of food and clothing and hunger walks abroad
unmolested. Only the workers can alter this. Against this
capitalist madness we pit the sanity of our demands: for
decency against destitution. Against the governments of the
capitalists we pit the mass might of the workers . . .*

   *The issue is not in doubt but work, organisation and action
are the triple points of our mandril guaranteeing 'these things
shall be'.* (MONMOUTHSHIRE HUNGER MARCH)

His sixteen page pamphlet of 1934, FROM EXCHANGE
AND PARISH TO THE P.A.C.: FOR DECENCY INSTEAD
OF DESTITUTION continues in this vein, still
attacking the failure of Labour councillors, in
this case of the Glamorgan County Council,
whose ranks, in opposition, he would join. There
is a reasoned analysis of the miseries undergone

by the unemployed in 1933 along with a firm reminder of how further concessions had been won by demonstrations and marches. Once more, though, it is the sense of forward motion that the pamphlet best conveys—progressive politics allied to the determination of workers whose spirit is not crushed as they emerge from all parts of Glamorgan to muster for the mass demonstrations at Cardiff. Small groups are seen coalescing despite all obstacles:

The first contingent started from Neath with a four days trek into Cardiff and no guarantees of food and shelter at any point. All day long the police at Neath had been conspicuously busy on the streets, standing in groups on corners, dashing about on motor cycles and in motor cars, visiting the women folk of the marchers with warnings of the consequences . . .

With a solitary drum muttering . . . Left . . . Left . . . in a monotonously throbbing undertone, the little band of delegates tramped their way through the tiny villages on the fifteen mile route to Glyn Neath, their first stopping place. . . . At seven o'clock, 2,000 workers lined the main street of this little township to welcome the marchers. The Town Band went out a mile or so to meet them. Everywhere was expectation. Half-an-hour, three-quarters—the workers waited, and still no sign. Then suddenly, breaking through the still night, came the rhythmic beat of a drum. From the darkened wood-enclosed road it came—louder and louder. When the band stepped in front, the drum ceased its cry of left . . . left . . . replaced by the strains of a spirited tune that gave new life to the men who had come so far on their way . . . Monday morning arrived, bitterly cold; but no one heeded it . . . In these two Rhondda Valleys were centred the main contingents and the backbone of the march . . . They marched down the Valleys picking up others . . . At Tonypandy a mass demonstration fell in behind the marchers, who had now been joined by the Caerau contingent. The four contingents converged at Porth and proceeded as one, with a living river of demonstrating workers, to Hopkinstown, where they were to join the other sections . . . The police attempted to divert the stream at Porth, but it was of no avail. The stream flowed on to its destination. Thousands of men and women took part at this stage. Shrouded in darkness, on a route lighted only by far-spaced gas lamps, the class fervour of the workers found expression in their lusty voices and tramping feet . . . Making the night echo with 'Arise ye Starvelings from your Slumbers', they forced their way along. (From EXCHANGE AND PARISH TO THE P.A.C.)

What marks this second passage out is the way in which the rousing bravado of the first pamphlet is complemented by the imagery of frail isolation becoming collective power—'solitary', 'under-tone', 'little band', 'tiny villages', give way to 'expectation', 'breaking through', 'spirited', 'new life' and, further on, neither 'darkened' nor 'shrouded' roads can prevent a 'living river', a 'stream' flowing to its 'destination' full of 'fervour' and 'lusty voices'. It is the feeling of the helpless finding a means, through togetherness allied to organisation, to influence their own destiny that Lewis Jones conveys. In the books, too, he will, in a quite unusual way, even for avowedly 'prolet-arian novelists', present a working class that, though formed by an inescapable reality, always has the means to re-shape their lives. He moves regularly away from abstraction to the concrete instance. In the middle of his January 1935 pamphlet/newspaper he addresses himself to the pitifully meagre pleasures that are barely available; and strains them through the sieve of his knowledgeable indignation:

Every summer, whatever the weather, streams of South Wales workers and their children leave their valleyed prisons and flow by bus, charabanc and train to the nearest seaside place some twenty or forty miles away. For this they save up pennies and threepenny bits throughout the year in club or chapel outing funds. Most of these 'savings' go in train fares, and food has to be carried in parcels or bags. But it is one day away from the misery. And what a day for the women! With the kiddies dragging around, crushed in the stations and on the sands, one eye on the children and the other on the food bag. Worrying and watching that the kids don't get lost. And at last back home worn out and tired. The day is over. Nothing remains but a bucket and spade, and a sixpenny 'while you wait' snapshot of the family. (SOUTH WALES SLAVE ACT SPECIAL)

Out of this deep political and personal involvement Lewis Jones now began to construct the novels that would serve him as a rounded means of combining the day-to-day actuality of South Welsh life over his lifetime with that lifetime's developed conviction that only self-consciousness in the individual and class-consciousness in the community would allow any species of real freedom. His two novels, in form and content, were to be a commentary on that charged history.

III

Although the idea of writing novels about a 'phase of working class history' may have been put in Lewis Jones's mind by Arthur Horner, this was no immaculate conception. A great deal of the strength of both novels, and particularly CWMARDY, rests on a firm, structured understanding of the history of South Wales as it had unfolded down to the mid-1930s. In a very real sense it was only from the vantage point of the mid-1930s that the patterns of that society could be traced back with some degree of certainty. By 1935 the forming shapes (in the union, in politics, in general outlook) of the world of CWMARDY were ossified or broken into shards. The novel is a closed one. Equally, WE LIVE is both open-ended and full of the vigour that stems from its main characters' hopes for re-shaping the world they have inherited. The paradox is that the second novel contains Lewis Jones's own recipe for social health through political vitality but that the first novel presents, with a devoted skill, a society, albeit less politically conscious, that vibrates with the novelist's traditional detail of life. If this is a fracture between the two books, and certainly it is a difference of style and vision that has divided critics, then it is no more than the society itself had undergone. WE LIVE, with its fierce, often schematic, tabulation of political lessons culminates in a wide acceptance of the logic of Popular Front policies impelled by the dynamism of a locally rooted Communist Party. It is a quite

34

remarkable piece of literature because, as Carole Snee has argued, it dispenses with the traditional presentation of individual character in the realist novel, as it must if it is to register Lewis Jones's understanding of South Wales as a place *essentially* revolving, by the 1920s, around collective, communal, and, finally, class experience. The skeletal form of the novel is a function of its anatomical purpose. In CWMARDY the skeleton is more slowly shown to lurk below the bones but it is always insistently, sometimes literally, there. John Pikoulis is right to point through Idris Davies, Alun Lewis and other coalfield writers, to the emblematic figure on the mountainside, the dreamer above the valley who, in Alun Lewis's self-chiding phrase, was always *enclosed . . . in an impalpable circle of seclusion, turning away to the Graig . . .* And Pikoulis is surely right, too, in his suggestion that the necessary removal, or distancing, of these writers from their subject—the people, the community—induces a psychological wrench that is akin to guilt. However, there is also the *literal* gap between the crowded, close life of the mining villages and the broad open moorlands just as there was, in more than one generation down to 1914, an actual divorce in the nature of a working life between immemorial, rural existence and a novel, industrial shift. Certainly in Lewis Jones's two novels there is little dreaming on mountain tops though he is not unaware of the symbolic possibilities implicit in the obvious, palpable co-existence of mountains and valleys. The novels have, then, to be seen, first as conscious end-products of the late 1930s, sure of their own political design for the coalfield, and, secondly, as fictional arguments for the absolute interaction of individual men and women with their moulding, collective history.

All of this is present in the opening words of CWMARDY:

> *Big Jim, known to civil servants and army authorities as James Roberts, stopped abruptly and let his eyes roam over the splendour of the mountain landscape. A coat hung uncouthly from his arm and a soft breeze played on the hairy chest that showed beneath his open red-flannel shirt.*
>
> *His small son, Len, stood near by wondering what had caused this sudden halt. He saw big Jim open his mouth as if about to say something, but instead of words came a smacking sound and a large mass of tobacco-stained saliva.*
>
> *The lad, whose wavy hair shadowed his sad eyes, watched the spittle twirl in the air before it fouled the grass at his feet. Len looked at the massive body that made his own feel puny, while Big Jim remained pensively motionless . . .*
>
> *'I be just thinking, Len bach,' he started, his deep voice tinged with pathos. ' 'bout the days long ago, when I did use to walk the fields of the North before ever I came down here to work in the pits.'*

Immediately we are confronted by the theme of both novels. On the one hand is the archetypal figure of Big Jim, the 'big hewer', whose bodily strength is starkly contrasted with that of his 'puny' son, Len, whose death is prefigured in his 'sad', 'shadowed' eyes and, soon, his 'plaintive' voice. Big Jim has brought his physical maturity to the pits; Len will mature within the society that is his from birth. These two will represent body and soul or rather, to re-word Marx, the 'people in themselves' who became, in Marx's formulation, the 'people for themselves'. Lewis

Jones's characteristic prose is also present straight-away. There is the keen ironic muscularity that distinguishes the demotic Big Jim from his officially baptised and registered self, and the quick deflation of Len's and our expectation when 'instead of words' comes the collier's familar, instinctive gobbing. With this sureness of thematic handling and ready juxtaposition of disturbing opposites comes a less welcome authorial voice that is strained, intent on showing its authority by speaking too directly for its characters (*His soap-stiffened moustaches gave him a fierce, reckless appearance which Len thought romantic*), and which is, above all else, hackneyed, imitative of an observed literary style. As with Thomas Hardy's less successful pages, the reader is compelled to swallow infelicities in order to take in the fresh-ness that is groping for an expressive style. It is no service to Lewis Jones to ignore or pass over defects of characterisation, of form and of style, on the grounds that the panoramic sweep of the novels excuses minor or incidental blemishes. These flaws are by no means only incidental. Nor do some quite major characters (Mary and Ron, for example, Len's wife and his friend) ever properly take on a fully developed role (either as individuals or as 'types'). The real objection to special pleading on behalf of Lewis Jones is that it diminishes his actual achievement by investing him with aims and successes he did not have whilst, at the same time, ignoring the way in which the force of his theme, and its attendant dramas of politics and work, breaks down the barriers of an arch literacy in its own stylistic interests. Certainly in the earlier novel he is necessarily at odds with himself from paragraph to paragraph. Len and Big Jim are still on the mountain:

Browsing sheep languidly chewed their way from patch to patch, while larks lifted their song into the blue recesses of the sky. Even the clear air conspired to produce an aspect of tranquil serenity on the mountain top. Rising and falling in tiny semi-visible globules of heat, the air played an irresponsible hide-and-seek with the bladed grass.

The two solitary humans were affected in different ways by the pacific scene. It softly recalled to the rough, toil-scarred miner the days of his youth. But young Len had no such solid memories to be awakened. In their place he felt a vague emotional hunger that made him sad. He turned on his stomach and lay full length on the grass before his father, who was meditatively moving a huge lump of tobacco from cheek to cheek, occasionally spitting its gravy-like juice into the air.

What saves the novel from the Arcadia tortured into being by the first paragraph is the linking sentence of the next whereby our central concern with human response is re-established. From now on, unremittingly, it will be the 'vague emotional hunger' of Len that will cry out for satisfaction as the boy confronts an array of problems and relationships that will go well beyond the usual journey from childhood to adult life without ever lapsing into an unimaginable sensationalism. In CWMARDY Len Roberts will be detached from the comforting satisfactions of his family by the horrors of sudden, unnecessary death (that of his sister in childhood) and then by the officially ordained miseries of a school intent on administering discipline for work not education for life. The glamorous world of pit life will give way to the drab realities of hacking out a daily wage.

The demands of the pit will become harsher as increased mechanisation leads on to speed-ups and the inevitable rise in the accident rate. When the men feel that their exploitation as a work-force by Lord Cwmardy can no longer be borne the strike spirals into a clash with the forces of the state, both police and troops. Lewis Jones correctly interprets the violence of 1910–11 as a catalytic agent in the politicisation of the colliers. Ezra is able to wield more effective power within the Union and to win a minimum wage (the scenario is precisely reversed in Llewellyn's HOW GREEN WAS MY VALLEY where it is political agitation that 'causes' the strike, and violence that leads to defeat). Len, helped by the grocer's son, Ron, who has gone away to college, picks up his lost education and deepens it by joining a Marxist discussion class ('the Circle'). Neither Big Jim, his lay-preacher butty, the beer-drinking, volatile Dai Cannon, nor the reluctant unionist, Will Smallbeer, are swept away by Len's changing perceptions. The early popularity of the First World War in the coalfield and the hysterical excesses of jingoism are not glossed over. The novel ends on a note of debate not resolution.

WE LIVE takes Len, just a little older than the century itself, into the sharpening conflicts of the post-war world. Despite his love for, and then marriage to, Mary, Ezra's daughter, Len's commitment to the youthful Communist Party is strengthened by the Party's analysis of events. Ezra is no simple betrayer of his class. He is, though, depicted as an outmoded leader. Eventually Mary and Len come to stand for all that is best and most selfless in local Communist

activities. Len's hunger is sated by conviction. He
is punished for his stand for justice by victimisation and imprisonment. The great strikes of the
1920s give way to the more localised, but fiercely
bitter, struggles against blacklegs, for the unemployed and, finally, the campaign in aid of the
Spanish Republic in whose service, as an International Brigader, Len dies. His death, however,
has been a chosen one. The second novel ends
with Mary heading a procession of people as Big
Jim and Len's mother, Shân, slowly bring up the
rear in a completion of the circle.

Len's death is, then, meant to signify a politically
fertile act. The last pages of WE LIVE are sentimental not so much because of their ring of
heroic self-sacrifice and the swelling chords of the
off-stage choirs of 'the people' but because they
project a political future which was, in 1939,
dependent on wish-fulfillment. The life can, in
this way, be justified by the death. Political
reality as it unfurls is, nonetheless, no respecter of
heroism. Lewis Jones had properly ended his story
with Len's departure for Spain. The book ends on
an upbeat note that may have served at the time
as inspiring propaganda but now sounds false
both as fiction and reality. The hollowness is
obvious when compared with the rich texture of
social and political life which Lewis Jones has
scrupulously erected around his main character
until his removal from the book. By that time,
Len has served his purpose as our guide through
the struggle of the 'living dead' of South Wales.
His, and Lewis Jones's, specific political conviction
is not as important as the process through which
he has arrived at his journey's end. Before that

journey could begin Len and his father have to
come down from the mountain:

*Len . . . let his eyes follow the sheep-track winding its way
down the mountain breast like a tortuous vein. He saw where
it buried itself in the murk and hid as if ashamed of its
eventual destination. It was just there, Len knew, that the grass
ceased to be green.*

*At last Big Jim knocked the burning ashes from his pipe
and rose to his feet. 'Come', he commanded the entranced
Len, 'I got to see Dai Cannon, my butty, so we will go down
the long way, past the pits'. Len followed obediently, being
always eager to get near the pit that stood at the top end of the
valley.*

IV

The fascination of the pit, depicted at first from the outside in a Lawrentian manner, is one that holds not only father and son in thrall. It dominates the village because it is the sole reason for the village's existence. After the mountain it is the first thing that we, like Len and his father, are made aware of—their bodies tingle and their flesh vibrates to its 'palpitating throb'. Its 'grotesqueness' in shape, its size, its smell, its blackness and immensity are the inhuman factors against which they will struggle. Lewis Jones's novels are not the simple, realistic chronologies he claims in his Foreword. It is the nature of relationships that is his true concern. To this end his text distills actual history to produce out of a multiplicity of events an essential, fictive pattern. In this way it is not only a public chronology that is distorted (a minor instance is the exact date of CWMARDY's beginning where the ages of Len and his sister do not tally with Big Jim's fighting the Boer War) but also a geographical narrowness that is imposed. Characters do leave the village but the important action all takes place within the parameters of Cwmardy itself. Leave alone the wider boundaries of Britain, or South Wales, the Rhondda Valleys themselves are not invoked beyond the immediate pit and its village. It is by focusing so sharply on the local, on individuals and on the detail of their lives that Lewis Jones manages to convince the reader of the sway of 'outside' happenings or the pressure of public, even international, forces on his chosen community. This is because no single life proves to be independent of others. The community of colliers and their wives instinctively know this yet it is only the revelation of this truth conceptually, in actual struggle, that allows the next step towards a class analysis of their lot to be taken. The position is put at the start of CWMARDY, in the mouth of Ben, the cynical witty barber whose shop acts as 'a local parliament'. Ben tells his customers they have *the real power in the world today* but stupidity prevents its use:

Here you are bragging how clever you are, and all you can brag about is how much work you do . . . Not a word about the money you get for the work! Now I know why you come to me on Sunday mornings for a haircut and shave on tick. It's men like you the masters want. Give them men with brains from their shoulders down and they have no need for any brains themselves . . . Huh, you make me sick.

Ben's sharp tongue is a goad but not a weapon. Lewis Jones refuses to allow this early statement to remove difficulties and produce enlightenment at a stroke. The internalised contradictions of his characters are material forces too. Knowing something to be so does not of itself lead on to a resolution. Lewis Jones balances on this dialectical tightrope, only occasionally falling into the impatient habit of forcing his ideal to break the stubborn complexities of his people's lives. Len is no mere cipher but he is deliberately given limitations as a character that allow us to share his concentrated obsession with the fuller lives of others, both in their actual living and their living potential. His life, and death, will literally be for others to have what, caught between the generations of 'people' and 'proletariat', he cannot truly have for himself. The political insight is Len's; the social and cultural matter of living is only his at one remove, in the rounded confusion of other lives.

Of no characters is this truer than Big Jim and his wife, Shân (in CWMARDY, presumably for metropolitan orthographic sensibilities, she is completely anglicised as 'Shane'). Big Jim is the first character we meet in CWMARDY and he is the last we see in WE LIVE. His 'magnificent body', which over a lifetime's work begins to waste, coupled to his status as immigrant to the coalfield where he lives with, then marries, Shân, presents the temptation of making him the People Incarnate. Lewis Jones does emphasise the sheer qualities of skill, endurance and compassion that Jim possesses in abundance. His real concern, though, is to depict Big Jim as an entirely representative type. So the big man is often insensitive to the needs and frailties of his immediate family, willing to make jokes at their expense and, on the spur of an adventure, to leave them, not just for the pub, but for foreign wars. He had, before CWMARDY begins, been a volunteer in the Boer War (sexual innuendoes and a reverence for military authority stay with him) and will, before its end, volunteer for the First World War. Big Jim's crudity is, nonetheless, a mark of wilful activity that Len envies. For Len sexuality will always be associated with death for, as becomes apparent, 'normal' human life will not be possible for him, or his generation. When Jim returns on

44

leave in the First World War he goes to the pub before he goes home and then, drunkenly, to bed with Shân:

It was many hours before Len went to sleep. Groans, grunts and creakings from the next room were hardly intercepted by the intervening wall. The sounds made him think of Mary, and again he felt the soft contact of her body, as he had felt it that day at the seaside. Little flushes of heat ran through his flesh at the memory. Then his thoughts turned to the bayonet his father had brought home. He shuddered as he recollected the rust on it, which he thought must have been blood. He imagined the point sinking into a man's body and the entrails being drawn out with the suction of the grooves at the sides. He felt a peculiar blood-curdling pleasure at these imaginings, but at last, with the creakings and groans still in his ears, he slowly drifted to sleep.

This animal vigour is a sharp contrast with Len's lovemaking with Mary in WE LIVE. Sex and death are intertwined here in the farcical illusion of life:

With excited haste he pressed her backwards on the bed and his kisses stole the blue from her lips, replacing it with a living red. Her head now rested on his arm and her flesh quivered with vitality as his hand sought its intimacy. Though neither spoke a word he saw the smile on her lips melt the shadows in her face before he clasped her to him and both were buried in each other.

Some time later, he turned on his side and carefully covered her with bedclothes, before drawing her body tenderly to his and stretching his hand to extinguish the light.

Their marriage will be childless. It is an insistent motif that Lewis Jones employs to keep Len apart from the majority rhythms of his society, and therefore, though all the more committed to 'the people' because of it, an observant outsider more than a full participant. His first sexual feelings have been aroused by watching his teenage sister, Jane, and the *death of Jane . . . marked the end of his boyhood*. She dies in childbirth bearing the illegitimate baby of the son of a pit official.

Her body was clothed in white lace and looked larger than when Len had last seen it. Her hands were waxy mirrors reflecting the blue tracery of all their veins. They were folded across her breast. One hand grasped a bunch of red roses that cast a blush over her smooth, white face, which seemed to smile into Len's downcast eyes.

Cuddled to Jane's side was the body of the baby that had killed her. Its tiny face looked like a blob of paste. Len felt a sudden urge to again caress Jane with his hands. He wanted to run them over the smooth contours of her breasts . . . he began to struggle hysterically in his father's grip. No tears came to his eyes as he continued the vain fight against Big Jim, but the feeling of impotence eventually conquered him . . .

Jim let him recover his breath, then slowly lowered him to the coffin until his lips touched those of his silent, smiling sister . . .

Five days after Jane had died Len was again taken in to see her. . . . As before, Big Jim lifted his son above the edge . . . Jane's beautiful face was gone. In its place was a dirty yellow mask with snarling lips that curled back from shiny white teeth. A blackened penny grinned at him mockingly from each of her eyes. The roses had died and were now withered blotches on the white lace of her shroud. Dark blobs filled the places where her cheeks had been . . . It made him feel sick.

This black, nightmarish comedy has two functions. It singles out Len's human response to what is unacceptable in human existence—he experiences the same 'mad' nightmares at school where his freedom is taken away and the pages of books become the thwacks of a cane, and in the pit where the increasing pace of mechanisation causes him to feel giddy and wonder if he is 'insane'. It is not, of course, Len's insanity that is in question. Big Jim and Shân, in a different way, are also able to make connections. Evan, the overman's son, is destined for better things than marriage to the pregnant Jane so, egged on by his parents, he denies his responsibility. In turn Big Jim rejects him as unfit to be even considered for a son-in-law and spells out the exact nature of the social difference between the two families. The overman, Jim contends, owes his job to the sexual favours he allowed his wife to bestow on the under-manager whilst his job, allegedly to watch for the men's safety, was, in practice, to force up the men's output. After Jane dies, Shân questions for the first time the justice of God. In both cases their rebellion is brief and primitive for it has no direction other than that given by grief and anger. For all that, it signals, too, the inadequacy and injustice of thrift, hard work and piety in staving off disasters.

The chapter that follows Jane's death is 'The Explosion'. What has been one, passing family tragedy is now turned into the constant, communal misery of pit deaths and accidents. In this case, conveyed by Lewis Jones in a chapter of swiftly moving, biting tension, the explosion and rescue attempts show the village united in the horror of mass deaths. The inquest, railroaded by a management who deny the real cause—

inadequate safety precautions whilst the rush for coal rules all—provides no justice from a jury with no miners on it. One who *is* on the jury is the shopkeeper Evans Cardi. He and his wife, dedicated to providing a future as a teacher away from the valley for their son Ron, will curse the strikes and impoverished times to come in WE LIVE. Their relationship to the community is revealed, without any harsh indictment, as dependently parasitical on the good opinion of the coalowners and even more so on the good wages of the colliers. Ron's defection to Communism is, in their eyes, caused by their own failure to maintain the cost of his studies. In a scene that is grotesque, if powerful in its dwelling on physical detail, the one-time juror clumsily cuts his wife's throat, with her prior consent, and then hangs himself in his own shop.

Their religiosity is falsely bound to notions of respectability. On the other hand, religious consolation within the community, from mass hymn singing to Shân's prayers for divine help, is not abruptly dismissed. In particular the lay-preacher-collier, Dai Cannon, who drinks nightly in THE BOAR'S HEAD, is portrayed with a great degree of subtle sympathy. The preacher is a part of the community and of its work-force. His instincts will ally him throughout to the struggle against the coalowners and the police. His oration at the funeral after the explosion, though questioned for its logic by Len, is clearly seen as a balm necessary for the grieving people in the face of these deaths:

His voice rose till it rang through the black air like the

wailing chords of a harmonium, 'O, Lord you seem so cruel to
your children this day. They, in their grief, do not understand
your infinite mercy and tenderness . . .'

'Give strength and courage, O Lord', he exhorted, his voice
falling in emotional waves upon the bowed heads of the
people, 'to those of Your children now suffering the horrors of
earthly partings from those they loved best. Give them solace
in their grief . . . Cast from the minds of these women and
children all thoughts of this week of death and devastation.
O God, we do pray Thee to sow again in our valley the peace
and happiness that we knew before the explosion.'

Those who listen weep in grief *and* in self-pity.
The only one who watches with 'hard and dry'
eyes, and with a cynical smile, is the miners'
leader, Ezra Jones, whom we have seen for the
first time at the pit-head after the explosion.
Ezra has no faith in these consolations. It is his
clear-eyed fortitude that makes him a leader.
At the same time, unlike Len, this inability to
weep, to share in the irrational part of human life
too, is Ezra's fatal, psychological undoing. He has
moved to the valley after leading a strike elsewhere. He was victimised. His wife dies, a victim
of prolonged semi-starvation. For all of this Ezra
blames the frailty of men just as much as the
ruthlessness of the masters. Ezra is a hardened
tactician of industrial strife whose strategy is
always bound by the framework of 'reality'. Len,
through the Communist Party, comes in WE
LIVE to challenge that pattern of victory or defeat
within acceptance of capitalism. First, though, Len
has to undergo the tortures and the comradeship
of the pit itself.

Although the pit is quickly, and rather conventionally, seen in Len's mind's eye for the monster against humanity that the school had been, it is crucial to note, too, the eagerness with which he goes down into the man's world of labour. This is, in part, Lewis Jones's sure handling of a theme familiar in many subsequent autobiographies and oral recollections—the first day underground of the excited boy-collier, all kitted up in white moleskins, eager to become a wage-earner. Even so, the matter of pit work, so abruptly distinct from surface life, tautens the prose of CWMARDY. Lewis Jones here finds less need to be tempted by abstract nouns or an occasional heavy-handed reflection because the specific account of life and work at pit-bottom can rely on little beyond his own memories. The writing is lucid, unaffected by literary models; we experience the pit's fatiguing work and its enticing novelties through the feelings, not the mind, of the boy-collier. The work skills of the miners, along with the clashes that arise with management, *at* the coal-face, are shown to be the underpinning of the solidarity that the whole community will demonstrate above ground. In the meantime it is Len's involvement in the pit's work and his simultaneous dislike of its demands on the whole of his life that Lewis Jones establishes:

The second day in the pit was much the same as the first, but this time he took more notice of what happened during the shift. When finishing time came he was even more tired and sore than on the first day . . . After dinner he fell asleep while he was bathing with his head over the tub . . .

In time he learned to hew coal and stand timber without the help of his father. He came to understand the struggle between himself and the coalface; and he pitted his brains against the strata, using the lie of the coal and the pressure of the roof to help him win the coal from the face with the minimum expenditure of energy. He learned the exact angle to stand his timbers so that they would bear the maximum weight of roof and side, and which part of the roof to shatter with a shot to bring only what he wanted to the floor.

In this manner, quietly and stealthily, the pit became the dominant factor in his life. Each morning, wet or fine, well or indisposed, he had to struggle out of bed at exactly the same time, join the never-ending silent flow of men to the pit, and travel the same ever-lengthening pit roadway. He came to hate the hooter, whose blast he had to obey if he were not to suffer loss of food . . . He saw the walk to the pit in the mornings as one long queue from which he dropped in the evening only to catch up with it again the next day. Slowly he came to regard himself as a slave and the pit as his owner . . . Not that he had any objection to the work, but the thought that he was tied to the pit horrified him.

It is this alienation that introduces, via some books from the student Ron, the abstract word 'socialism' into CWMARDY (about a third of the way into the novel). From now on Len's distaste for the monotonous regularity of pit work grows. Lewis Jones, however, holds a delicate balance between Len's utilisation of genuine pit grievances in order to agitate amongst the colliers for industrial action (in both novels) and the men's irate contempt for management's profit-squeezing.

Jim started to his feet . . . but the fireman, exasperated by his failure to get the men back to work, interrupted, 'Hell fire! Do you 'spect me to shit bloody timber for you?'

51

A voice from outside the circle of light shouted: 'No. And even if you did it 'ood be no good to us, because nothing from you would be of any use to anybody'.

That contempt, felt equally by Len, may fuel political struggle when it is thwarted but its origins lie in the pit community's own sense of justice. Len's return to work after a long lock-out in WE LIVE is a categorical acceptance not of the necessity of work but rather of the change in him effected by work.

The 'bang . . . bang—bang' of the wooden droppers falling into place as the cage dropped out of sight sounded strange to Len and the hot, foetid atmosphere of the pit, after the long period of fresh air on the surface, made him choke. He tasted it thick in his mouth and retched like a man who had never been down a pit before [but] . . . He felt glad he had been destined for the pit and laughed at his one-time longing to be freed from it. The dangers and the struggles, the hatreds and the humour had become part of his life. His body and mind had been moulded in the pit by his fellow workmen, and without them he knew his world would be empty.

This, in turn, makes the men possessive about the pit. Not for its profit making nor the intrigue of the mysterious but for the fact that they have made it just as much as it has enveloped them. Big Jim, the old-fashioned craftsman, is astonished on his return to work to find that he is to be directed to work wherever management decide. He wants to work his own stall. The fireman tells him

It is not your place any more than it is mine . . . All the pit do belong to the Company and they can do what they like with what they own, can't they?':

'Not my place?' Jim challenged. 'Who the hell drived it in? Who ripped it down and timbered it?' His voice became shrill with thwarted pride. 'Who risked his body and slogged his guts out to keep it tidy so that there was always a tram of coal ready on the road and two in the face? Not my place indeed. If it is not mine, who the bloody hell's is it?'

The control, limited but real nevertheless, that a collier like Jim had had over his own work before 1914 has vanished with the increasing organisation demanded by the owners and their officials. His individual pride must go the way of his craft. What is not lost, amidst the anger, is the human solidarity induced by pit work:

Len had been silent throughout this argument, although he saw the new tactics the company was adopting to break the men apart and scatter them among neutral strangers in various parts of the pit. He caught his father by the arm.

'Come on, dad. There's nothing for it but to go where we are sent.' Jim looked like refusing, but after a brief hesitation he responded . . .

. . . Jim walked up to the man who was working, at the same time tilting his lamp so that the light fell full on the stranger's face.

There was an awkward pause while Jim scanned him up and down before asking heavily: 'What for did you come here and work another man's place, butty?'

'What else could I do? I either had to start here or not at all.'

'That's right, dad. It's not his fault', Len broke in, fearful that the old man would lose his temper again.

Jim sighed . . . He turned to the stranger and advised: 'Take care how you do work that face, butty. It is hellish funny and you have got to keep your butts clean and cut the right-hand side in front of you all the time if you want to work her as she ought to be worked. And you want to watch the top.

It is very sly and you can't trust to test it with a mondril, because it will ring like steel one minute, then, before you can blow your nose, it will drop 'bump' like a shower of lead . . .'

The man thanked him . . . and the couple, sharing the tools between them and bent double beneath their weight, left him . . .

The slaves of the mine are, in work itself, gradually reduced then, as Ben the barber had prophesied, to mere hands. What he had failed to see was that their reduction to less than their self-estimation would be the trigger that would set off a larger capacity for self-release. The same is true of the counterpart to the pit, the village. Here a community grouped around chapel, home, pub, square, fountain, and shops, the bare elements of a civic life, discovers it is the prisoner not the keeper of its own environment. At first (by 1912) there is the sheer scale of new, booming enterprise that lends a gloss to the grimmest environment:

The village was now more prosperous than it had ever been. The pits never ceased their throbbing night or day. The 'foreigners' had inter-married with the natives, their children now young adults, creating a new cosmopolitan population in the valley. Street and mountain fights were no longer so frequent, but the continually extending police station housed more police than it ever had. Each of the four groups of collieries had its separate federation lodge, linked together by a Combine Committee. Mr. Evans Cardi, together with most of the other little tradesmen, extended their premises and their business at the same time. A new theatre was built near the square. Every Saturday the men and women of the village followed their rugby football team into the neighbouring areas, and the game sometimes turned into a battle of fists. A new railway was laid through the valley to deal with the flow of coal that was too great for the railways already there, and

54

the city by the sea into which this coal was poured became one of the greatest ports in the world. Beautiful houses and buildings sprang up in it. The number of its millionaires increased with the increased number of ships that left its docks with coal for the four corners of the earth. Lord Cwmardy became so wealthy that his daughter could afford to travel the country demanding rights for women.

Lewis Jones rarely writes in this sweeping explanatory mode. To do so would be to lose the weight of his close investigation of a felt, community life. It is a necessary distancing point, however, on occasion, for it establishes that the 'natural' rhythm of Cwmardy's life is actually drummed out by the pit's throb. The fight that will come for control of pit life is, then, not an incidental in the attempt to win control over all other aspects of the peoples' lives. Lord Cwmardy, whom we see briefly, in his big house at the valley's end, accepting the pressure of the banking houses to cut the colliers' price lists, understands this logic and how his new economic activities will smash an older community pattern. He is seen, in cameo but not as a caricature, dreaming sentimentally of the *gymanfa ganu* over which he will no longer preside. That is at the start of WE LIVE, set in the early 1920s. The community, under the accumulating pressure of long-term poverty, can no longer sustain the oddments of behaviour that amounted to respectability and deference. Debts and bankruptcies take their toll. Evans Cardi and his wife frame the impossibility now of holding such a view of community, and of living on without illusion. Their suicide occurs in their empty shop, its shelves and their larder bare, yet in spite of extreme poverty, *their pride had forbidden the sale of any of the furniture, each piece of which they regarded with an affection second only to that which they had felt for their son. The various wooden articles filling the home symbolised for them the stages and episodes in their married life, and they now reminded Maggie of the past.*

There is no salvation available for these two. Their relationship to the community is a mechanical, clockwork one so the slump leaves them with their springs broken and Evans Cardi's body swinging *like a pendulum on the rope.* The community itself is already groping a way towards self-definition. In the days that lead up to the General Strike of 1926 (with the deaths of the grocers as a part-consequence) the distinction between the miners' class interests and those imposed on them is spelled out. It is not union or political figures who do this for their role in the novels is to explain how to mobilise feeling. Lewis Jones has a representative of the older, pre-1920s culture voice the threat in WE LIVE:

A murmur rolled round the room, and one old man who was the founder and deacon of one of the local chapels, rose to his feet. Even above the subdued whispering, his chest could be heard rattling like a bag of marbles. Numerous blue scars were scattered over his hands and face like tattoo marks, but when he spoke, his voice, though hoarse, carried a timbre that made it sweet in the ears of his listeners. Job Calfaria, as he was known to the workmen, had won the respect of the people by his devout efforts throughout his life to practice in the pit and in Cwmardy the principle he preached each Sunday in the chapel. He was now tremulous with emotion as he said.

'Twenty years have I waited for this. Twenty years of work and pain. I have seen butties go one after the other down

56

the hill to the cemetery, each poorer after all he had done than when the good Lord first sent him into the world. And now, when my race is nearly run on this earth, what I have prayed for so long is about to come. Oh, my fellow workmen, how glad I am to know that these old eyes of mine will see you free and happy before they close forever on the sins of our masters.'

. . . The murmur that had preceded his speech now became a rumble of sharp claps and stamping feet that brought the meeting to a close.

Twenty years would take Job's audience back to the days immediately preceding the explosion and the strike that had erupted over the issue of non-payment for small coal. That, in turn, had made the men unite in a demand for a minimum wage. The whole episode, towards the end of the first novel, is crucial in demonstrating to the people of Cwmardy what exactly they can and cannot do. Len's politicisation and Ezra's acclaim as a leader are rooted here. More than that, Lewis Jones, with the mid-1930s firmly in mind, alters the actual historical events in order to convey an undercurrent of popular power.

The initial tactics of the strikers are to prolong the strike, so hitting at the owners' profits, by preventing all work in the pits. Natural justice is the defence of all their actions. The officials and blacklegs who try to work are forcibly prevented. Their homes are daubed in black letters—'blackleg' or 'scab'. The success leads to the importing of police which bewilders everyone (except Ezra). Dai Cannon explodes:

'But they have no bloody right to bring police in from outside. The duty of the police is to stop stealing and to catch

murderers. Nobody is stealing here and nobody have yet been killed. Whoever asked for them to come here had no bloody business to do it. We know how to carry on a strike without interference from outside.'

The new police hassle the people about the streets until a mini-riot is provoked by a baton charge. Within a few days further clashes prove inevitable

It was a matter of honour to the people in the valley that the Square belonged to them and that no one could turn them from it

as the strikers, by instinct, reassemble. Lewis Jones sketches the separate small-group existence that makes up a crowd with great care. The people are not a mob. When mounted and foot police attack the crowd of thousands he sets out, in dramatically packed narrative, the ability of the massed people, when provoked, to crush the police:

The sweeping suddeness of the attack disorganised the police, who ran like rabbits for refuge in the neighbouring side streets. But here women were waiting for them with buckets of water and slops, which they emptied on to them from bedroom windows. Gradually the police were driven from the Square, which was left in the possession of the strikers.

For a short while after this the strikers prove, through subsequent battles with the police, that they are in control. The control allows feelings of revenge and the requirement of social justice to surface. In a scene reminiscent of the sexual humiliation meted out to a shopkeeper who has given goods for sexual favours in Zola's GERMINAL, Evan the Overman is singled out by the crowds of men, women and children who march purposefully to each house. Shân, in a symbolic gesture often adopted by colliers' wives during these disputes but given extra poignancy in the novel by earlier events, has Evan held down whilst she covers him in the dead Jane's night-dress:

'Proud man you did ought to be today, Evan, wearing my Jane bach's night-dress. Let your eyes see it. Don't it look nice and white and clean, like her little body did be before you and yours did send it rolling to the grave . . . You do 'member, Jane bach, don't you, Evan? She did used to pass your house to chapel. Yes, of course, you be bound to 'member her.'

When Evan made no reply she changed her line, 'Look you, mun,' she rasped through her teeth, 'what revenge you have now. Often have your wife's night-dress covered the naked backside of Williams the manager; today Jane's do cover your body over your clothes.'

Lewis Jones's accuracy in depicting the total involvement of women in the struggle is not merely an exemplary piece of documentary reportage. Contemporaries were worried that women did not, in fact, accept the roles designated for them by the imagery of woman as meek, domestic help-mate. At the root of their concern was that the division of authority, of which the division of labour and of sexes was an integral part, would not be sustained. Lewis Jones is not afraid to hammer home working-class blindness in these matters. Indeed, one of the outstanding features of both novels is the full, sympathetic treatment of women that has about it no hint of patronage or sidetracking.

Len talks to Mary after the women have been demonstrating against blacklegs:

'I am not much of a scholar since I left school, but the strike is teaching me a lot of things I would never have learnt without it. The boys in work talk of girls as the owners talk of us. The owners make us slaves in the pit and our men make their women slaves in the house. I've seen my father come home after a week's work and chuck his small pay on the kitchen table, chucking his worries with it at the same time. My mother had the job of running the home and rearing him and me on money that wasn't half enough to pay the bills . . . A man's worries finish in the pit . . . I have heard my butties talk about women exactly as if they were cattle—to be taken up the mountains and then laughed at in the pit . . . [but] Look at our women today. They are on the picket line with us, they are in the riots. It is they who give our men the guts to carry on . . .'

This world-turned-upside-down, the very stuff of popular disturbance, cannot survive the intrusion of a greater reality. It now comes in the form of a repressive state apparatus that sends troops to control uncontrollable, self-controlling CWMARDY. Once more the two forces come together and this time the Riot Act is read before eleven strikers are shot dead. It is the first major shift from the actual course of events. In Llanelli in 1911, at the end of the national railway strike, troops killed two men and wounded five others but no-one was ever shot in the coalfield itself. After the fictional incident Ezra's quest for compromise to avert further miseries is over-ridden by Len's eventual plea to fight to the end. Within a couple of paragraphs, and following the continued terrorising of officials, Lord Cwmardy, *in the tenth month of the strike . . . grimly announced that the men could restart as soon as they were ready and that the government was introducing a minimum wage act . . . News of the victory was conveyed to the people at a mass meeting on the rubbish dump where they had first declared for strike!*

Now the actual sending in of troops by Churchill, the Home Secretary, in November 1910 (not the idyllic summer weather Lewis Jones has pulled in from the lock-out of 1926) prolonged the Cambrian Combine strike, effectively ensuring the return of the mid-Rhondda miners in 1911, after ten months, on the terms available to them before their strike began. The Minimum Wage Act of 1912 only appeared in the wake of a British national strike. Lewis Jones's fictive rendering is, therefore, of great interest in assessing his purpose. He is concerned, in 1937, to depict not only the fate of people in armed struggle but also the long-term effects of their willingness to grapple with the state. He wants to lay bare the underlying sinews of coalfield life from 1910 to 1937 rather than its silhouette. Therefore the people are shown as first the innocent victims of police brutality, though treated by the newspapers as aggressors, then the righteous avengers who beat back the police from *their* town, actual restorers of self-control over their civic life, and penultimately, martyrs. He proceeds to telescope the process of advance and retreat that marked South Welsh industrial strife from 1910 to 1921 by having the men assured of justifiable victory.

A number of things can then flow from his re-telling of events. These factors are self-evident to Lewis Jones in 1936 even if they did not happen in the manner he suggests. The first is that Len's stubborness in the face of overwhelming odds is made more 'real' (i.e. it works!) than Ezra's pragmatic caution. The second point is that this confirms Len's faith in the people as a body who are never self-betraying in contrast to Ezra's stated position of contempt for people who will raise up and bring down leaders on a whim. Thirdly, Ezra's understanding that the men's committee can only function if it is truly representative of demands conceived in the pit itself (where power truly lies) is allied to a drive for a permanent organisation, 'the federation'. Once again there is a vital inversion of order. No mention is made of the existence of the South Wales Miners' Federation from 1898, nor the district unions that existed before this, nor of the contemporary debates raging within the SWMF over centralisation and the accountability of leaders. Non-unionism was a severe, long-standing problem before and after 1910. This is the messy chaos of an actual history whereas Lewis Jones writes to highlight the evergreen potential of a rank-and-file people who require union organisation *after* they have acted, and won a victory. This alters the more complicated history of the SWMF without distorting the dialectical relationship between a working class, its self-activity and its required organisations. He is right, too, in this stress on the Federation as the body around which political life based in the working class will form. Ezra will now represent Cwmardy on the Federation and on the council.

The pit which we have encountered at the start

of Cwmardy in its guise as monster is, in its moulding of community and individual, also a creative force. The industrial and political victories at the novel's end mark the way in which men and women can use its sullen power for their own good. For Ezra this is a matter of riding the tiger, of moving with 'fate'. For Lewis Jones the lessons of strike and organisation have brought in yet one more, the need for complete control of 'fate.' Cwmardy ends with Mary for once agreeing with Len that

'*We are ourselves responsible for what happens. The pity is that we follow events instead of trying to determine and mould them. Our fate is in our own hands.*'

Already Len had begun to study Marxism, though Ezra's disapproving contempt (and prior knowledge of Marx) had discouraged him. Lewis Jones moves Len onto the path of political progression, away from his mentor Ezra, by first having him experience (rather sketchily through denunciatory speeches) the capitalist causes of the First World War and, then, more sharply, by plunging him into the dangerous speed-up of the newly mechanised pit in a post-war world. Control, he begins to see, cannot be sporadic if it is to cease being erratic. Len asserts

'*. . . if our people have the power to win strikes even against bullets and batons they have the power to do away with their poverty, to put an end to the struggle and begin to live . . .*'.

We Live continues Lewis Jones's delicate probing of the life-experience and self-contradictions of a working-class community in South Wales. For all that, its principal thrust, one that often alters his style and his form, is linear not referential. The second novel resolves those contradictions by concentrating on the political growth of Len, Mary and their 'people'.

V

At first glance it is CWMARDY that echoes the novel's formal tradition—replete with the stuff of life, taking a sensitive character on an odyssey of discovery. WE LIVE, on the other hand, can be said to break with this chiaroscuro style by playing a blinding light on collective or mass history and by emphasising *its* prior claim on our attention. Nonetheless, Lewis Jones interprets history, through his drama of representation in CWMARDY, in such a way that we are forced to consider the play of society on individuals. In the first novel his own ideology works to derive fictional insight from the interaction of his imagination on his, and a collective, memory. There was little contemporary written history which he could study. Ness Edwards' HISTORY OF THE S.W.M.F. would not appear until 1938; David Evans's 1911 compilation LABOUR STRIFE IN THE SOUTH WALES COALFIELD is a loaded piece of reportage to which Lewis Jones's 'fictional' account of the riots serves as an instinctive antidote. CWMARDY works imaginatively against the grain of history precisely in order to give meaning to the lives of the community it interprets. WE LIVE, set over the twelve years of Lewis Jones's active political life from 1924 to 1936, is so sure of its historical facts that they can be totalled up in an overwhelming political argument. This is a retreat into naturalism, albeit of a collective variety, not the full advance into a realist tradition that CWMARDY so tantalisingly promises. The gain is a novel able to dissect South Walian industrial conflicts and politics from the inside; the loss is, with a number of episodic exceptions, the working-out of change and growth both within individuals and their society. In place of this Lewis Jones too frequently offers his main characters rhetoric, abstract arguments, dialogue that abuts in the political message we are supposed to grasp and, naturally, there is the 'people' who are, in the Depression years, shown to be without any hold on life apart from mass activity. They are there, with due humiliation, to be led. They are there to inspire the weary leaders. As Len tells Ron:

'Keep close to the people. When we are weak they'll give us strength. When we fail they'll pick us up and put us back on the road again.'

They are there to justify the childlessness of Len and Mary who offer themselves, through the Communist Party, as agents of future regeneration.

Len caught her arm and pressed it to his body. 'Never mind, comrade', he consoled, both himself and her. 'If we can't create anything with our bodies, we can with our minds and the work we do for the Party. That's something to go on with isn't it?' . . .
'I was thinking of all the little kiddies who think so much of us. Of how they rush to us when they come from school and shout "Hallo, Len. How be, comrade" before asking for fag photos. They are so true . . . when we go, what will they have to remember us by? Nothing, Mary. Nothing, except the fact that they once knew a man who had always been unemployed— a man who wandered from meeting to meeting and street to street always looking for something he never seemed to find.

Ah, but now? When they look back . . . they'll be able to say: "We knew Len. He fought for us in Spain, and Mary helped him." Yes, my love. How much better a memory is that than the deadness of the other. It will help them when they are men and women to be active in the fight. That's what we want, activity that leads to action, not the inertia of pessimism and despair. And what our children see us doing, they do later for themselves . . .'

'Who knows? Perhaps, when they look back on the past, they'll be able to brag to each other: "Our Len died in Spain." '

The trouble with this ending is not that Len and actual volunteers went to fight, courageously, in Spain out of a confirmed political logic but that the character, Len, is made to embrace death as the last fruit he can give to Cwmardy. In fact his own life has become subordinated to that of Mary (in the Council, leading women against the Means Test, becoming the local party organiser— *She was her husband's superior intellectually, having the capacity to think more coherently and feel less acutely . . .*), to an Ideal of the People (*'it is only by our love for the people that we can measure our love for each other'*, he tells Mary), and to the role of catalyst in public incidents. Death *is* his logical political end for he has only a limited connection with the diurnal life that continues to be lived in Cwmardy, both in actuality and in fiction. Len assumes the mantle of universality that drapes the enlightened. Doubts fall away from him, irony does not dog his footsteps so that, casting no shadow, he floats free of our engaged interest.

Before this happens, before the epithets limp after the abstract nouns into the dying sunset, Lewis

Jones wrestles his characters into political consciousness through the twists of events. For Len,
however, it is only the refinement of an already
acquired political credo that happens since he has
joined the Communist Party on the night the
novel begins. Politics, as defined by Harry
Morgan, the local Party leader, have become the
most important thing for Len. Even so, Lewis
Jones, without ever mounting a formal criticism
of the Party, is at pains to stress the links between
the past as represented by Ezra and the future as
seen through the eloquent Harry Morgan. Their
connection is emphasised by the hatred and
detestation of both by Fred Lewis, who brags of
his early membership of the Party and regards
himself as a 'foremost theoretician' yet truly
despises 'all other men' as 'nincompoops' to be
led by the nose. Ezra and Harry, in contrast, are
both men of principle. Their mutual opposition
is a pre-condition to a new phase of the workers'
struggle. The locally imposed lock-out drags on
for nine months until Ezra, pleading the semi-
starvation of the village and the danger to the
preservation of the Federation, agrees unfavour-
able terms to allow a return to work. Ezra is
given powerful words to argue his case but it is
his weakness and lack of faith in 'the people'
that is stressed. What is of particular interest here
is the suggestion that a 'non-political' union is
already in formation and ready to oust the
Federation. Lewis Jones knew of course that the
actual non-political union (the South Wales
Miners Industrial Union) grew and survived in
the coalfield after 1926, in the wake of the General
Strike, until 1938. Yet he introduces it *before* the
men's resolve is broken and *before* any species of

defeat is imposed, so that Ezra can be shown, in accepting the terms, to be pre-empting the non-political union. The old leadership of the Federation is already partially discredited. Ezra himself is now an arch-conciliator wrapped up in the guise of William Abraham ('Mabon', President of the SWMF from 1898 to 1912) whose phrase 'half a loaf is better than none' is attributed to him.

Ezra remains the dominant force in the politics of the pit and the village. For a while Len and the Party are forced into acquiescence. They do not wish to prolong any disunity amongst the men, who have indeed followed Ezra's line. Len even wonders about the Party's original stubborness in opposing Ezra. The fact that Len is now married to Mary allows Lewis Jones to bring the political disagreements between the two men, with Mary arguing first one way then the other, into the second family situation in Len's life. Conditions in the pit worsen, 'strangers' are employed and the native inhabitants drift into long-term unemployment. Ezra becomes a JP and is now opposed by the Party for his seat on the council—

Len . . . found that the struggle against his father-in-law widened his ideas and gave him a better appraisal of Socialism and all that it meant. The old illusions bred in him by Ezra and later by Fred Lewis, regarding revolutions and politics, were shattered, and, altogether he gained a basis of knowledge that made him an able lieutenant for Harry Morgan and a formidable opponent for the miners' leader.

The tandem ride continues, however, for Ezra is still a shrewd, formidable leader able to act with dispatch and correctness on a number of issues. The inescapable conclusion, though, is that he cannot use these gifts beyond the trade union. His politics is a hopeless brand of evolutionary procrastination. Only the Party prepares to develop working-class confidence in the approach to the 'Big Strike'. The 1926 General Strike is skirted over quite abruptly. Its end is announced by Len as a betrayal 'by a small group of politicians who call themselves leaders of labour'. Len, himself, has been absent on Party business, agitating elsewhere, during the Strike. Once more it is not the issue of the General Strike within British politics after 1918, nor its half-cocked outcome, as part and parcel of the direct action/ syndicalist theories in circulation since 1910, that gives Lewis Jones any pause. The episode is trotted on and off only in order to affirm the correct analysis of the Party (betrayal as inevitable) and the revolutionary potential of the misled masses.

By this time we are locked into a game of political shuttlecock whose outcome Lewis Jones, from the Popular Front niche of the late 1930s, is anxious that we see:

In the meantime [as the lock-out continues] Len had renewed his boyhood friendship with Ron, and they spent hours together discussing how the Labour Party could save the position through Parliament and the council. The discussions sometimes became very fierce, when they differed on matters of policy, but always they met again to pursue the argument. Len was adamant that no solution to the troubles of the people could be found through Parliament . . . :

'You can depend on it, nothing will ever come to us except through the trade unions and revolution. The pits and factories are the fortresses of the working-class and only through them will we free our people.'

Ron was equally adamant that if the Labour Party worked correctly and sincerely in Parliament there would be no need of a revolution. 'Before you capture the pits', he asserted . . . , 'you have got to capture political power.'

This always stumped Len, particularly if Ron accompanied it with a challenge. 'After all, isn't your Party a political Party, striving to organise the masses to take power out of the hands of the capitalists?'

This is a neat tying together of revolutionary syndicalism, extra-parliamentary action and the establishment of political power at the heart of the system. Len goes to jail because he is involved in a demonstration against the local 'insincere' Labour council. Ezra, with the Federation breaking up, feels constrained to take a clerical job in Lord Cwmardy's office. It is Len, though, who pushes hard to reorganise the Federation rather than merely concentrate on the Party's line of organising the unemployed. Lewis Jones squashes together the whole disputatious phase (1927–33) that was marked by outright Communist Party denunciation of the SWMF as a 'scab union' and characterisation of the Labour Party as 'social fascist'. He leapfrogs, via the instincts of Len (here adopting attitudes and policies that led the Party to accuse their principal Union spokesman of the 'aberration' of 'Hornerism'), the abyss of meaningless politics in which the party argued for the imminence of outright revolution. It is the Party's role as inheritor of the right to lead and guide 'the people' that Lewis Jones is keen to stress.

Ezra, whose disgrace has been defended only by the forthright words of Big Jim, dies on a high note, urging Len and Mary to fight for the living since

'It is the flesh and brains of our people that gives life to the world. Without them the world is dead . . . fight for them . . . Fight, fight, and keep on fighting until . . . '.

Ezra's death allows the baton to pass to the Party. It is the Party, with Harry Morgan down from London, that organises the funeral. His coffin is draped by a red flag 'with a gold hammer and sickle emblazoned on its centre', and carried by six old Federation committee members and six Party members. By this ceremonial sleight of hand Ezra, the staunch anti-Communist and Labour Party councillor, is turned into Ezra the genuine political warrior of the past who can be engrossed into the authentic political future. Big Jim and Lord Cwmardy head the procession to the crematorium where Harry Morgan speaks to punctuate the symbolic grammar of a passage in the novel that has operated as a wilful short-cut through the political maze of the 1930s in South Wales:

Harry Morgan went to the pulpit and . . . he began the people's farewell to Ezra. He pictured Ezra's life as steps in the struggles of Cwmardy, each incident and action irrevocably leading to a certain outcome.
   'He weakened at the end!' he declared, 'but which of us dare say we would not do the same in similar circumstances? He failed to see the struggle as a river flowing on against ever stronger dams placed there to stem its progress and divert its path. He took our people through many of these dams, but

reached one that could only be broken through by a collective leadership, by a revolutionary Party that, knowing the strength of the obstacles, could mobilise the people into a unity powerful enough to overcome all barriers. Our Party did not regard Ezra as an enemy. We loved him for what he had been and what he had done. We grieve for him today, but we also glory in the knowledge that the foundations that he laid are safe in the keeping of the Party and the people.'

The remaining third of WE LIVE is a rapid, almost cinematic, coverage of the stirring fight back within the SWMF, of the actions taken against the Means Test regulations and on the political front. Throughout, by no means without a large measure of justification, the Communist Party is put centre stage. Mary becomes the moving force as befits the daughter of Ezra and the wife of Len. Having been elected to the council she argues in the party cell for unity on the council between Labour and Communist councillors just as unity exists, she argues, within the Federation against the 'non-pols'. What is not said is that it was previous Party decisions to replace the Labour reformists which had mostly led to the bitter disunity. The unity is cemented in joint agitation against the cuts in unemployment benefit. The result is a chapter ('Cwmardy Marches') that recounts the enormous, and successful, monster demonstrations in all the South Wales valleys, in early 1935, that were largely responsible for ensuring the National Government froze its new Unemployment Act. Irrespective of the accuracy of Lewis Jones's retailing of the origins of these imposing, communal protests (and his constant, yet half-hidden, references to the Combine Committee of the Federation suggests that he

was well aware how mobilisation of the re-
organised SWMF was crucial since, no matter
how ardently local Communists worked, nothing
on this scale was conceivable in *that* South Wales
without the Federation), it is his marvellously
resonant insistence on the power that can only
be derived from a collective presence which
make these pages so thrilling. The organisational
structure of 'unity' is the one Mary sees, signifi-
cantly, as 'the cure, Len, for me and the people',
and it is absorption by the people that inspires
Len who

*felt himself like a weak straw drifting in and out with the
surge of bodies (until) . . . something powerful swept through
his being as the mass soaked its strength into him, and he
realised that the strength of them all was the measure of his
own, that his existence and power as an individual was buried
in that of the mass . . .*

This mystical fusion may well be the nectar that
these two require to avoid individual isolation
but even more important, quite unique in fact
in the canon of political working-class novels, is
Lewis Jones's central thrust against both Ezra and
Big Jim's earlier fatalism—the people can cause
change, can control matters without that control
being only the momentary one following a riot
or the passive one of dogged survival in a pro-
tracted strike:

*When the front of the demonstration was two miles advanced,
and on the summit of the hill to the east of Cwmardy, people
were still pouring from the assembling field. Len lifted his
head sharply into the air when he fancied he heard the distant*

74

strains of music in the direction left of the demonstration. He
turned to Mary and the workman next to her.

'Can you hear anything?' he asked.

They both looked simultaneously past Len, and he, seeing
their amazement, turned his head to look in the same direction.
He drew his breath sharply and his perspiring face went a
shade whiter. The mountains which separated Cwmardy from
the other valleys looked like a giant anthill, covered with a
mass of black, waving bodies.

'Good God' the man next to Mary whispered 'the whole
world is on the move.' . . . she murmured, 'No, not yet. But
the people are beginning to move it now.'

The chapter ends, after a stirring invasion by irate
women (led by Mary) of the Unemployment
Assistance offices, with an invocation of Unity
which, in effect, has returned the vitality of
self-direction to a battered community. The
optimism that was working like a yeast through
the traditional working-class institutions of South
Wales after 1934/5 gives the novel a surging
uplift. A continued rate of non-unionism, one
that left half the work-force outside the Federation as late as 1935, and the running sore of mass
outmigration do not merit a mention. Lewis
Jones has, from the start of CWMARDY, been set on
hauling the possibilities for human life that
Cwmardy possesses across the ruins of communal
destruction. He has referred to the economic
disarray of the coal industry and the political
strife that smashes up all manner of social and
political certainty from 1918 to 1933 only in
passing. What he has wanted us to see is how
these terrible matters have destroyed illusions
and lives only to end with the greater lessons
that a unification of Communist theory and

mass practice can produce. The play or third novel that he meant to write would, it seems, have projected a socialist future.

Prior to Len's departure for Spain and martyr-dom, however, Lewis Jones settles his book back in the pit from which, as in his real world, so much human pride in solidarity was derived. Two superb chapters dramatise the late 1935 stay-down strikes in which colliery after colliery, in a wave of semi-organised and mostly quite spontaneous revolt, saw its work-force go on strike under-ground until non-unionists and company union men (the 'non-pols') were removed. In some pits, notably the company-union dominated Taff Merthyr, the two unions co-existed after an SWMF strike had won the right to a free ballot in 1934. This, and some later incidents from 1937, are lumped together somewhat indiscriminately by Lewis Jones who also has Len suggest the whole idea in a secret Party meeting. Again, though, it is the pounding drama of a work-force who find their own power in a disciplined, collective style that he concentrates on to good purpose, building the tension of the unfolding of the secret plot with a masterly ease that seems to be his every time the far-away people become the closely observed colliers and their wives. Big Jim's rough, salty tones, sadly missed in the cut-and-thrust of Len and Mary's righteous discussions, illuminate the scene more powerfully than ever, especially since he, too, is now more politically aware. That awareness, in him, is not the abstract melting into the people of the swooning Len. Big Jim's every movement, word and deed carry, with total conviction, that personification of a people into a proletariat that Lewis Jones urges too desperately on us at other times.

The men, in Lord Cwmardy's angry words, cannot be allowed 'to confiscate the pit'. In the context of the novels they have done far more than this. Their occupation of the pit implies control of everything above the pit as well. When Len goes down to assess the situation he, touchingly, insists on his right to join in but, firmly, they send him away:

'Where is Len's place, boys? Up or down?' . . .
  'Up' came the unhesitating response . . .

And down there his work mates, now in the pinpoint, accurate detail of life observed (and imagined of course), re-create, out of the matrix of industrial and class struggle, a fragmented sense of a community. Concerts, eisteddfodic competitions, agreed sharing of duties and of food, discussions and adjudications do more than while away the time in the pitch dark, they present these men with the light of a microcosmic experience of corporate identity. They grow closer together when no news comes down and the promised food fails to appear. The dialogue ranges from solicitous affection to a raucous spatter of leg pulling and comradely bawdy that brings to mind the defiant concentration on the 'trivia' of humanity that his contemporary, John Ford, brought to the cinema. They shared in common that poetry of the mundane more than they diverged in their overt messages. The following is typical:

*Will Evans stumbled and crawled about until he found Big
Jim. 'Something must have happened on top, James, or Len
and the boys would have grub down long ago.'*

A loud grunt and a movement prefaced Jim's reply.

*'I could fancy my back is broken, mun, but there . . . what
do backs count if the heart is good.' . . .*

*. . . A loud shout interrupted the conversation. It ran
through the stable like a wail.*

'Can't anybody stop this bloody snoring by here?'

A number called out: 'Get to sleep and forget it'.

*'Sleep to hell. How can a man sleep when that bloke makes
me think the missus is in bed with me?'*

*More joined in. 'Watch him, boys. If he's got strength to
think of his missus in bed, he must be picking grub from
somewhere.'*

'Order, boys. What time do it go dark?'

*The question was answered by a chant: 'It never goes dark
till your eyes are shut.' Everyone joined in this, after which
there was quiet for another spell.*

*Jim took advantage of this to whisper. 'I'll go back to the
pit bottom to see if there is any news . . . '*

'I'll come with you' Will replied.

*'No, no! You stop by here to make sure that nothing out of
the way do happen. If anybody say they are thirsty or hungry,
let them chew timber.'*

*Back came the retort: 'If us chew much more timber,
munniferni, us will be shitting sprags.'*

The stay-down strike continues. That, in itself,
has re-asserted the sense of control over their
destinies which is its true victory. The problem of
resolving the strike, of holding on to its emotional
energy without losing the more obvious prize its
courage has brought within the Federation's
grasp, remains. In the 1930s both the Labour
leadership of Jim Griffiths (SWMF President

1934–6) and of Arthur Horner (Communist President 1936–47) negotiated the Company Union out of existence, after intense struggle, by compromise. This muted, but successful, tactic was loudly denounced at the time for its apparent vacillation. Lewis Jones, in a delicately poised scene, depicts Len, at the meeting called by Harry Morgan to end the strike, as torn between obedience to the Party's line, strongly supported by Mary, and his instinctive reaction. The Party's view is that the strike must end since its division of the work-force, above and below ground, threatens disunity and 'anarchy'. Harry Morgan, and Mary, believe the Party, now elected to office, *must lead in everything that concerns the pit and the Federation.* Len, swallowing the self-directed jibe of 'strike-breaker', forces himself to speak in Morgan's support. His speech, though, is more effective in its denunciation of the owners than it is convincing in its logic which acts, via Mary, as a check on *any tendency to irrelevant wildness on his part.* For once Len's oratory, ended 'abruptly and unexpectedly', leaves *the people in a welter of surprise and conflicting emotions . . . clammy with disappointed expectancy.* Lewis Jones has delivered us, and Len, to his disciplined political conclusion. The novelist, no less than the hair-trigger rebel, cannot leave his subject there—*The meeting continued in an atmosphere of dull apathy for some time, but it ended in an uproar of dissent and indecision.* Len 'became sad' because he felt driven to make the Party's appeal whereas Mary had been, earlier, 'nervous' since she feared *her husband's vehemence when he felt a thing deeply.*

The dilemma is more than a tactical one. Len has arrived at a personal impasse. He has to be right *against* his work mates. The burden is almost insupportable. Lewis Jones now squares the circle by having management invade the pit in an aggressive attempt to force the men up. Resistance and capture of the manager ensue so that Lord Cwmardy caves in by agreeing to the right of free choice over joining a union. Nonetheless, there is no written agreement and management save face by having the men ascend the pit before one is drawn up. The Party line, then, was implicitly wrong because neither side had exhausted its strength. The strikers will only accept Len's word on the granting of the ballot. Once this is given they prepare to leave the pit. They do so by leaning on each other and refusing all aid or provisions from the members of the deputation.

'There is not enough for all of us' said one as he rejects the offer. 'And we might as well stick it till we can all get some.'

'Aye' said another, 'and we have had to depend on ourselves all this time, so we might as well depend on each other now at the finish.'

The chapter ends with the imprisoned strikers welcomed into the sunlight of their release by waiting friends and relatives:

When the first carriage full of strikers banged its chains against the droppers, the rush of released air was smothered in the terrific cheer that rolled and crashed over the valley. Police and officials were scattered about like coaldust when they tried to keep the people away from the pit head. The strikers were tenderly lifted out of the cages and tended by loving hands while they waited for the remainder to come up. Kisses mixed with happy tears and both were lost in the

singing and cheers as the cage slowly emptied its final load.
The last man to step out was Big Jim whose trembling hand
arrogantly twirled his long moustache. Shân rushed towards
him:

'James, oh James bach', she sobbed, as she flung both arms
around him and pressed her face to his black one when he bent
down to kiss her. 'I knowed everything 'ood come all right.'

He raised his head and seeing Mary nearby, stretched out
his hand affectionately to stroke her brown hair glistening in
the electric lights.

No one ever remembered exactly what followed, everything
was excitement and tumult. But the blare of a brass band took
command of the situation, and, in step with its lively march
rhythm, the people took their victorious strikers down the hill to
Cwmardy, where banners and streamers waved a breezy
welcome home.

We do not see Len. We do not need to see him.
The pit work-force has been re-united, the
community given a sharper class focus, Big Jim,
Shân and Mary given each other in an understood, common fight. Lewis Jones affirms in the
stay-down scenes, and in their victorious end, the
resurgent humanity of his people. The message
is one that came to sound sentimental in the
darker 1940s and too vibrant for the muted
aesthetic of the 1950s and 1960s. There was,
however, a stunning compulsion in the diagram-
matic map of the coalfield's history that we are
given in the novels. A rediscovery of that history
allowed a fuller appreciation of the novelist's
hypnotic achievement. We understand the force
of argument which takes us from the forming,
'syndicalist' society of CWMARDY through the
travail of struggle, towards the understood,

'communist' destiny implicit, and finally invoked, in WE LIVE.

What will give CWMARDY and WE LIVE their continuing interest as novels, however, is not their declarative statements of intent nor their acute documentation of a melodramatic political history nor even their bold invention of individual characters who take all the elements of an active life from those around them. The novels will live because, in addition to all the formalist and historical interest they possess, they partly succeed in resolving a dilemma that runs like a geological fault through European prose fiction. The success is only partial. Lewis Jones does occasionally fall into the trap that in 1931 Georg Lukács (ESSAYS ON REALISM, 1980), had seen as marring the proletarian novels of Willi Bredel— that of distorting the revolutionary process so that *the revolutionary line always prevails against the trade union bosses,* and of adopting an *abstract treatment of language* that leads to *absurdity and kitsch.* At the same time Lewis Jones follows Lukács in the latter's insistence on the depiction of *obstacles, difficulties and setbacks in a display of dialectical thought [that] dissolves the rigid appearance of things . . . into the processes that they really are.* Lewis Jones adds something, too, that is neither a mechanistic imposition nor an ectoplasmic subtlety. His major achievement, in politics and in the novel, was to refuse to divorce the way people rightly want to live, fully, in their only present, through all its cultural and material confusion, from an equal commitment, however fragmented it might be or become, to a control of their world that might allow an even more human future. He lived that belief. He wrote of such lives.

Bibliography

LEWIS JONES

Novels

CWMARDY, London: Martin Lawrence, 1937, pp. 310. Republished, Lawrence & Wishart, 1978.

WE LIVE, London: Lawrence & Wishart, 1939, pp. 334. Reprinted in A Worker's Library, 1941. Republished by Lawrence & Wishart, 1978.

Short Stories

'Young Dai', DAILY WORKER, 1 July 1932.

'Power of the Pit', DAILY WORKER, 23 August 1932.

' "Boots, Shiny, Big and Heavy . . ." ', DAILY WORKER, 28 April 1933.

'The Pit Cage', DAILY WORKER, 21 June 1933.

Pamphlets and Miscellanea

MONMOUTHSHIRE HUNGER MARCH OF AUGUST 1933, Abertillery, 1933, pp. 15. Written and Compiled by Members of the Monmouthshire Marchers Council. Foreword by Lewis Jones.

From Exchange and Parish to the P.A.C.: For Decency instead of Destitution, Tonypandy, 1934, pp. 16.

'The Rhondda in 1934', Daily Worker, 19 May 1934.

South Wales Slave Act Special, Tonypandy, 1935, pp. 8. Published by Lewis Jones for the South Wales N.U.W.M.

'Tonypandy', Left Review, April 1937.

'Tory Coalminer', Left Review, August 1937. Review of *Coal Miner* by G. A. W. Tomlinson.

Biography

Idris Cox
Entry in Dictionary of Welsh Biography, Cardiff, 1959.

Hywel Francis and David Smith
The Fed: A History of the South Wales Miners in the Twentieth Century, London, Lawrence & Wishart, 1980.

David Smith
'Leaders and Led' in Rhondda: Past and Future, Ed. K. S. Hopkins, Rhondda, 1973.

'Tonypandy 1910: Definitions of Community', Past and Present, 87, May 1980.

Anon.
'A Revolutionary Writer', WELSH REVIEW, Vol. I, June 1939.

J. H. K. Edwards
'The Life and Works of Three Anglo-Welsh writers of East Glamorgan', M.A. Thesis, University College of Wales, Aberystwyth, 1962. (unpublished)

John Field
'The Archetypal Proletarian as Author: British Coalminers as Writers', LITERATURE AND HISTORY. Forthcoming.

Philip George
'Three Rhondda Working Class Writers', LLAFUR, Vol. 2, No. 3, 1981.

Monica Hassel and A. Cim Meyer
'Literatur Og Politik: En analyse af Lewis Jones's *Cwmardy* og *We Live*', Thesis, University of Roskilde, 1981. (unpublished)

Glyn Jones
THE DRAGON HAS TWO TONGUES, London, Dent, 1968.

Ramón Lopez Ortega
LA CRISIS ECONOMICA 1929 Y LA NOVELISTICA DE TEMA OBRERO EN GRAN BRETANA EN LOS ANOS TREINTA, Salamanca, 1974.

Movimiento Obrero Y Novela Inglesa, Salamanca, Universidad de Salamanca, 1976.

'Industrial Conflict and the Viewpoint of the English Novel in the 1930's' in Gulliver, iv., Berlin, 1978.

'The Language of the Working Class Novel of the 1930s' in The Socialist Novel in Britain: Towards the Recovery of a Tradition, ed. H. Gustav Klaus, London, The Harvester Press, 1982.

'The British Novel of the 1930's and the Working Class: Notes for an Introduction' in English Literature and the Working Class, Universidad de Sevilla. Forthcoming.

John Pikoulis
'Lewis Jones' in Dictionary of Literary Biography, Ed. Bernard Oldsey, New York, Bruccoli, Clark, Gale. Forthcoming.

David Smith
'Myth and Meaning in the Literature of the South Wales Coalfield: the 1930s', Anglo-Welsh Review, Spring 1976.

Introduction to Cwmardy (Yr Academi Gymreig Reprint), 1978.

Introduction to We Live (Yr Academi Gymreig Reprint), 1978.

David Smith
Socialist Propaganda in the Twentieth Century British Novel, London, Macmillan, 1978.

Carole Snee
'Working Class Literature or Proletarian Writing?'
in CULTURE AND CRISIS IN BRITAIN IN THE THIRTIES,
ed. Clark, Heinemann, Margolies and Snee,
London, Lawrence & Wishart, 1979.

Randall Swingler
'An Epic of the Rhondda' (review of WE LIVE) in
DAILY WORKER, 19 April, 1939.

Raymond Williams
'The Welsh Industrial Novel', Cardiff, University
College Press, 1978.

'Working Class, Proletarian, Socialist: Problems
in some Welsh Novels' in THE SOCIALIST NOVEL IN
BRITAIN, ed. H. Gustav Klaus.

'Realism Again' in NEW SOCIETY, 20 November,
1980.

W. H. Williams
'A Working Class Epic' in LEFT REVIEW, vol. 7,
August, 1937.

Acknowledgements

A number of people have helped me to think, research and write about Lewis Jones. In particular I would thank Hywel Francis for sharing an obsessive interest with me since 1968, and for facilitating my use of the Lewis Jones Collection (diaries; obituary notices; pamphlets; newspaper reviews; tape-recorded memories) housed in the South Wales Miners' Library at Swansea. My gratitude, for their inspiration and encouragement, goes to Ramón Lopez Ortega, John Pikoulis, Gwyn A. Williams, Tim Williams and N. A. Wyson.

I am grateful to Lawrence and Wishart for their permission to use extracts from *Cwmardy* and *We Live*.

This book is for Lyn Thomas in memory of Gwyn

The Author

David Smith was born in Tonypandy in 1945. He was educated in the Rhondda and at Barry Grammar School. After reading History at Balliol College, Oxford, he researched for an M.A. in Comparative Literature at Columbia University, New York, and for a Ph.D. on the interwar history of the South Wales coalfield at University College, Swansea. He has lectured in Modern History at the University of Lancaster (1969–1971) and at Swansea University (1971–1976); since 1976 he has been in the History of Wales Department at University College, Cardiff, where he is now a Senior Lecturer. He has published numerous articles and essays on the social history and literature of Wales, Britain and the USA and is a co-author of both THE FED: A HISTORY OF THE SOUTH WALES MINERS IN THE TWENTIETH CENTURY (1980) and FIELDS OF PRAISE: THE OFFICIAL HISTORY OF THE WELSH RUGBY UNION (1980), which won a Welsh Arts Council Prize in 1981. From 1973 to 1981 he was joint-editor of LLAFUR: THE JOURNAL OF THE SOCIETY FOR THE STUDY OF WELSH LABOUR HISTORY; he introduced and edited A PEOPLE AND A PROLETARIAT: ESSAYS IN THE HISTORY OF WALES, 1780–1980, (1980). David Smith lives in Pontypridd.

This Edition,
designed by Jeff Clements,
is set in Monotype Spectrum 12 Didot on 13 point
and printed on Basingwerk Parchment by
Qualitex Printing Limited, Cardiff

It is limited to 1000 copies of which this is

Copy No.   979

British Library Cataloguing in Publication Data

Smith, David
    Lewis Jones.—(Writers of Wales ISSN 0141-5050).
    1. Jones, Lewis, *1897-1939*—Criticism and interpretation
    I. Title   II. Series
    823'.912   PR6019.0

    ISBN 0 7083 0830 9